se·ques·tered

SE·QUES·TERED

/səˈkwestərd/

JOEY TRUMAN

Whisk(e)y Tit

VT & NYC

Every word of this is true. However, names, characters, places, and incidents are reserved as possible products, in part or in full, of the author's imagination, and should not be confused with your idea of reality. Resemblance to actual persons, living or dead, events, or locales is entirely coincidental.

Published in the United States by Whisk(e)y Tit: www.whiskeytit.com. If you wish to use or reproduce all or part of this book for any means, please let the author and publisher know. You're pretty much required to, legally.

ISBN 978-1-952600-09-8

Copyright ©2020, the author. All rights reserved.

Cover design by Michael Jung.

First Whisk(e)y Tit paperback edition.

DAY ONE

A dream come true. No work. No one insisting I go to work. Rock gigs, cancelled. Reading gigs, cancelled. All social engagements, cancelled. Lie around all day. Cooking. Reading. Every prediction I made over the last three years coming true. Rent paid for the next three months. What else? What else!

Travel, cancelled. Subway, cancelled. A world focused on the crisis it should be focused on. An unjust economy. An unjust healthcare structure. An unjust wealth disparity. Stocks crashing. Airlines/Fossil Fuels/Insurance. Moral pariahs. I mean, if we can't stop the stock market from crashing, even with all the things we have in place to prevent it from crashing? Airplanes and Global Warming? The Fossil Fuel industry? I mean, it is true that shit rolls downhill, but what if we just get out of the way and let the shit roll all the way to the bottom and let it stay there?

Three bags of black beans. Dry. Three bags of pinto beans. Dry. Five lbs of bacon. Froze. Twelve pounds of potatoes. Bagged and stored. Twenty rolls of toilet paper. A bag of flour. Yesterday I made an Irish Dinner. Corned Beef and Cabbage.

> Corned Beef and Cabbage
> Buy Corned Beef in a bag. That is something that your supermarket has for some reason that you never really understand why, but you are aware of. In a bag. I mean, pre-packaged. It comes with spices. It is a little like bacon in the sense that somebody cures it for you. I mean, how many times have you had an Irish Dinner? Without being Irish? In Brooklyn? In a Black/Latinx part of town? My answer is: Once. Last night. Professor Curly is Irish/Jewish. Curly red. Skin like white onions. A smell that will water your eyes like white onions too. Just joking. She has a squirrel that runs around her neck. Me? I am German, maybe? Dutch? The census came on Friday. I didn't know how to answer that question. Mutt.

There is no real recipe for this meal. Buy meat. Buy cabbage. Canned beets, apparently. Boil everything for three hours. Eat.

It's not bad.

Oh, and potatoes. And carrots.

But let me tell you about the mood right now. New York is on lockdown. Everything is depressed. There is a lack of joy. Uncertainty. We all know that something is coming, but we don't know what. The enemy is invisible. I made the mistake of comparing the feeling to right after 9/11. My friend Josh got mad at me. He said it was nothing like that. He told me a story about how he was on a train after 9/11. There were all sorts of pictures taped up inside the train of missing people. He said that he looked over at a woman crying on the train. Then he looked at another woman on the train, and she started crying. Then another woman on the train started crying. Eventually every woman on the train was crying. I am not saying it is like that. That is not my point. My point was that it feels like something sad is happening and we can't quite wrap our minds around it. We are trying to go about our daily lives, but it is really difficult to know exactly what to do.

We also know that the government is lying to us. That we are on our own. That the shit hit the fan and is a boomerang and will hit the fan again. That we are now in a recession. That this recession will turn into a depression because none of us are financially secure. We can't stop working for a week. We can't. We will be bankrupt. Two weeks? Six weeks? Through summer? But what do we do? Schools are closed. Bars. Restaurants. The Met Gala. There are one hundred thousand kids in our school system that are homeless. 50% of the kids that go to school depend on school lunches and breakfasts for most of their caloric intake for the day. Rents in New York are insanely expensive. Everyone who is rich and white enough will just leave town because they have somewhere else to go. The rest of us will just stay here and starve to death, I guess. Get evicted.

I say that like I have a problem. I don't have a problem. For once in my fucking life I am prepared for this. It's an accident, kind of. I have been saving money. By accident of timing the lease that me and Professor Curly signed is up for renewal. And because we paid four months of security deposit we can apply that to the new lease starting May 1st. Which means free rent until August. But work is cancelled for the foreseeable future. I went to the bank today and took out $600 dollars just in case. I don't mean to be paranoid, but if the Federal Reserve dumps $1.5 trillion dollars into the bond market and it does nothing to stop the Dow Jones from taking a nosedive…and then they tell the banks that they don't need to have 10% of their assets in cash any more and they are free to just lend money to whoever without oversight, I don't know. I feel like that might undermine the FDIC, and the small amount of money I do have might not exist tomorrow. Not that paper money will be worth anything at that point, but I would like to think I did a smart thing right before everything went to shit.

I think I will do it tomorrow too. I could have gone into the bank proper and emptied my account, but I didn't want to have contact with other humans. Which is kind of ridiculous considering I used the money machines. But I have a way of dealing with cash in these tumultuous times:

Iron Your Money

Money is 75% cotton and 25% linen. There is a small chance that the Coronavirus is heat sensitive. If it is, well. Iron your bills. I wore gloves when I was doing this. Use the Cotton/Linen setting. The highest setting. Iron for thirty seconds per side. Place in a Ziplock bag when finished. Store somewhere with sunlight. Like near a window. Southern facing.

I am not advocating for panic. Don't go empty out your bank accounts. I just get nervous when I think about the fact that we have a President in the White House who has no problem using bankruptcy insurance to solve his idiotic business decisions and we are now living off of credit cards because his tax breaks for the rich don't generate income for our tax system, and now that the markets are crashing and we have no money coming in and we can't pay the money back and we have been borrowing from the Chinese for the last however many years and they have gotten the Coronavirus under control at this point, and we haven't, we will be severely weakened by our inability to pay back our loans and therefore…

If I was China, I would tell America to go fuck itself.

But you should probably have some cash on

hand. Just in case. If the FDIC bonks, you will at least have one last good and tasty meal before you have to eat worms from the sidewalk. But remember to iron it first.

Iron Your Money.

DAY TWO

Professor Curly gave herself a haircut. I gave the vacuum a haircut. We used the same scissors. I mailed in the 2020 Census form. Professor Curly filled it out. Better handwriting. Jess and I finished the last edit of Etiquette. Via Google hang. Sent the cover details to Murphey. Well, photo and font ideas. Made a second St. Patty's Day dinner. Professor Curly is eating it now. Probably watching **The Office.** I am doing some laundry in the bathtub. Bought a six-pack of Guinness.

Oh! did some bonin' on the couch. Started with a bj by the front window. Then a cop showed up.

There is a pigeon turd on the window that looks out into the courtyard from the bedroom. I might clean it tomorrow. We are starting a regimen. They say this could last through the summer. Supposed to go to Wyoming in a couple weeks. Think the trip is cancelled. Professor Curly had to cancel a trip to Los Angeles next week. She spent a couple hours trying to get in touch with the airline today. Nothing doing. She will try again tomorrow.

My daughter is now going to school from home. Via Zoom. Whatever that means. Three classes in the morning. An hour for lunch. Three classes after. Tomorrow she has P.E. [Physical Education]. Also, show and tell. She is bringing her cat, Shiver.

My brother, who lives in Portland, Maine, works for a brewing company. He says they are stopping keg production and focusing on cans and bottles. Going to do a curbside delivery thing. He said that our home town, Worland, Wyoming had their annual NRA [National Rifle Association] gathering yesterday, even after being warned against it. Not sure who he heard that from. Probably one of our brothers.

Made a tuna salad. It was pretty tasty. Used a bread called: Milk Bread.

Tuna Sandy with Choppers:
   can of tuna in water
   chopped celery
   chopped sharp cheddar cheese
   chopped onion [red]
   chopped jalapeño
   chopped garlic
   mayonnaise [2 tbsp]
   mustard [1 tbsp]
   salt and pepper
   2 rolls of Milk Bread

Open tuna. Drain. Mix everything together in a big bowl. I suggest you mix the tuna and mayonnaise and mustard together first. That way you can add salt and pepper to taste. But it is not necessary.

Toast Milk Bread.

Put half of mixture on each roll of Milk Bread.

Serve with potato chips [plain] and a little dish of catsup. For dipping. Professor Curly drank a diet soda instead of the dipping catsup.

Call your family. They are worried.

DAY THREE

Saw a car crash today. Same place I saw one a few weeks ago. A car and a minivan. The car t-boned the minivan. Last time the minivan t-boned the car. Nobody was hurt. The funny thing though. Last time I was about three blocks away before the emergency vehicles showed up. Really fast. This time. I was able to walk to the bank and back. Forty-five minutes. This time they were still waiting for the cops and ambulance to show up. Resources I guess. Or lack of resources.

Took more money out of the bank. They halted trading twice today. The bank itself was closed. Until further notice. The poor and the elderly are the first to suffer. They are also the last to stop suffering. If at all. It's not like they are phasing us out. Right?

My new flip-fone sucks. But at least I can get emojis now. Thanks for the upgrade. Can't wait to have to join social media in order to get paid in the future. Even poverty can't save you from the slavery of corporations anymore. At least I get paid a living wage and have health care as a trade off for sacrificing my freedoms.

At least I am clean. They can't take that away from me. They can take the gas to make it warm. The apartment I live in. The electricity I need to survive. But at least water is free.

Water is important. I like water. It is tasty. Quenching. Useful. You can freeze it if you have electricity. Boil it if you got gas. Store it under your bed if you have an apartment. And a bed inside that apartment.

Made a pizza today. Deep dish. Kind of. The dish wasn't deep enough for the small amount of dough we had. Pepperoni. Onions. Jalapeños. Pickled garlic [gift from Christmas]. Couldn't get yeast at the grocery store. They were out of flour tortillas too. Everyone is walking around half annoyed and depressed. Part paranoid and exhausted. This is no snow day. Regardless of what the mayor says.

Called my mom. She says not much has changed in Worland. Schools are closed though. She laughed when I asked her about the NRA.

Been listening to Deep House. Dance music is nice.

Don't know what to say about the economy crashing. I know that lots of people have money tied up in the stock market. 401(k)s and such. But what can I say? The stock market has always been immoral. Rich assholes playing poker. What happens when the delusion that is the construct of money collides with the reality that 2/3rds of that money is connected to workers who live paycheck to paycheck and can't go to work anymore? If they can't buy what you are selling? Cars? Houses? What if it is rent? Food? Subway fare? Let alone computers and phones? Pants? They say they are gonna give people $2,000 dollars. But how? To who? All the people that need it won't get it. It will go to the middle class. Who don't need it. Yet. There is no way they can just send out cashier's checks to whoever is just hanging around. Like the way the Census works. They won't just send out, for instance, three checks to this apartment building. To whom it may concern. How will it work? You will have to be in the system. Paid your taxes. Et cetera.

And right now. Right now? We are just at the beginning. Sitting around doing nothing. Eating food all day. Biding time. What happens two months from now when the economy really hits the skids? That $2,000 dollars will be worthless. You either saved it because you didn't need it, or you spent it on useless junk from Amazon. Either way it just goes to the top and doesn't help people that actually need it. People that already needed it. Like the poor. The kids that have to go to school to get breakfast. Lunch.

What we need to do soon, and now, is to start food banks in the center of every city and town in

America. A place to go and get free food. Suspend rent. Utilities. And not in a way that needs to be paid back. No bridge loans. All debts suspended. School or otherwise. Grocery delivery for the elderly. Mass transit fares must be suspended. Subsidized laundry. Free laundry. And soap. Toothbrushes. Toothpaste. Paper towels. Toilet paper. Clothes drives. Donations. A large cauldron of tasty vittles on every corner. Free for all.

All of it. Everything that is a tax on the poor in normal times should be free and available right now! For anybody who needs it.

If we can spend fifty cents of every tax dollar on the military in order to build $200 million dollar drones that get shot down in Iran on accident and nearly start a third world war, we can get together and help the poor in America. We can also scream at Congress to lift sanctions on Iran so they can deal with this crisis too. Before millions of people die for no reason.

Ugh. Bummer.

Follow me on TikTok.

DAY FOUR

XXXXXXX

DAY FIVE

Buy gold.

Who could have predicted that income inequality combined with a succubus corporate business model combined with stagnant wage growth and a lack of health care could have wreaked so much havoc on an economy that depends on spending from 2/3rds of the population? This is insane! It came out of nowhere!

In the best of times this model is barely functioning. The economy is great! For who?

There is this exchange from the movie *The Day After Tomorrow*, which is a movie about climate change and the disaster that will unfold when it gets past the point of no return. The point of no return. I don't know how to word this. When things become irreversible and can't be fixed. It doesn't matter. I hope you know what I mean. But the scientist character, Jack, is giving a speech and the Dick Cheney character has some questions:

"But this would cost the world economy billions

of dollars. I think you should consider that before you make such sensationalist claims."

"With all due respect, Mr. Vice President, but the last chunk of ice that broke off was about the size of the state of Rhode Island. Some people might call that pretty sensational."

The cost of doing nothing.

Buy gold.

Free Bernie.

Bernie Madoff is the Robin Hood of our generation. The only thing he is guilty of is wanting to live a lavish lifestyle. Which is something that I, personally, don't aspire to, but I won't fault him for it. And conversely, I don't think that means he should spend 150 years in prison.

What did he do exactly? He preyed on the greed of wealthy people. And it wasn't that difficult. Pretty funny how all you have to do to dupe somebody is to tell them they are making money with their investments even when they aren't. Making money, I mean. If you tried that on a poor person you would last about a month before you were exposed. Hey, that thousand dollars you invested in my scheme is now worth two thousand dollars! Okay, great! I need a thousand back so I can pay my rent. Keep investing with the other thousand dollars! About that...

Let your money work for you.

Invest in copper. They say that the Coronavirus

can only live on copper for 4 hours. 48 for cardboard. 48 for stainless steel. 72 for plastic. Hours. I don't know how long it lasts on gold. But that doesn't matter. You just bury it in the backyard. For the next time.

I don't know. I grew up poor. I know exactly how much money I have at any given time. Spoiler alert. Not much. And I don't think the people responsible for this crisis that we are going through understand that thought process. Money is not abstract when you are poor. It is very physical. Papers. Coins. I didn't lose a single cent as the stock market crashed. Crashes. And I never will. Because it is immoral and frankly evil. But I will suffer its effect. I already am. I am out of work. It is pure luck that I have savings. They won't last. I give it two months before I lose all this baby weight I have been storing since the fall. Then what? No jobs. Even the jobs that were supposed to be the last resort jobs, the fast food/dishwashing jobs don't exist anymore. Yes, the economy is important, but fuck you! the economy is really important! But not in the way you think it is.

Hourly wages are not an abstraction. People live on that shit. Those wages. Not teenagers. Families. There is no fucking bridge loan that will make the crushing weight of poverty go away. A bridge loan for somebody that can't work and can't bring money in is just debt. More debt. Debt you can't get out from under. Debt that will stay with you for your entire life if you don't pay it back. Like student loans. Do you not understand why you can't declare bankruptcy on student loans? I will tell you why you can't. It is simple:

Moral Value

If you can't pay the loans back to the government that lent you the money, that means that the money they lent you is a Subprime Loan. And if that Loan is Subprime, that means that the government shouldn't have lent you money in the first place. Therefore, forgiving those loans means that those loans are bad loans and are therefore, invalid. Meaning! the cat was dead the whole time! Don't look in that box, Professor!

If I had student loans, which I don't, college didn't make sense twenty years ago, and it doesn't make sense now, I would feel zero moral obligation to pay them. Go to a technical school! Learn a trade! Liberal Arts? Fuck you! Lawyer. Teacher. Start a hot dog stand. I can't think of anything dumber than going to college.

Nerds!

Unless, science. Math.

If you can't come out of four to six years of schooling and make at least $65,000 dollars a year, the first year, you are a fool. And Bernie Madoff gets 150 years in the clink for tricking millionaires into believing that they are making money when they are not, just so he can have a nice house and nice suits?

Fuck that!

¥

I made some flour tortillas today. Not sure if they are any good. Professor Curly seemed to like them. I guess I will try them when I am done here.

The grip tightens. I think we will be on full lockdown starting Sunday. Not sure what that means. No walking around, maybe? Buy groceries? Maybe. Trains stop running? Buses? They say that Americans don't like Pinto beans. This is good for me. I like Pinto beans. All those empty shelves except Pinto beans. Beets though. Can we just throw those in the trash? Save us all the trouble? Professor Curly had me buy some Oat Milk today. The only carton, half-gallon, that was left. Extra Creamy. Ew. If you want something extra creamy, Babe!

Okay, hold on. Let me dissect those last four sentences:

1. The last half-gallon of Oat Milk was extra creamy. Ew.

2. Professor Curly can suck a dong. Wink.

3. Becca would appreciate that joke.

4. Mushrooms.

Later days. I will leave you with a good quote:

"Is this dying? Is this all? Is this what I feared

when I prayed against a hard death? Oh, I can bear this! I can bear this!"

— Cotton Mather, New England Puritan minister and author (13 February 1728)

DAY SIX

Professor Curly got it. Then she didn't. Turns out she was just exhausted from worry. Took a nap. Ate a cupcake. Right as rain.

The sky is crazy. No planes. No pollution. It's like the city quit smoking. Enjoy it while it lasts. I guess I'll look up tonight. Maybe I can see stars.

I am worried about getting enough Vitamin B. Or REEB, as Cara Tobin would call it. I think everything will be shut down by tomorrow. Except grocery stores and pharmacies. Not really that worried, actually. Been meaning to start working, Bone Dry, as they say. When opportunity knocks, knock back. Knockers.

New York City Guidelines For The Covid-19 Pandemic: Wash hands before bonin'.

The flour tortillas taste like soda crackers. Saltines. Soft Saltines. Not bad, but not really what I was going for. Guess I will give it another go.

Took a nap today. Baked a chicken pot pie. Packaged. Had a spice that tasted like mold. Turmeric.

It was 75F yesterday. Will get down into the thirties tonight. Snow on Monday. Supposedly. Think there was maybe one snow this winter…all I remember was a dusting and a flurry. Crop dusting. One time I called my brother Luke to complain after a pretty girl crop dusted me on the street, and he said:

"Pretty girls fart too."

I don't think I was calling him to get advice. But like they say, Don't ask questions you don't want the answers to.

DAY SEVEN

Dumped a cupcake on my keyboard. They are boarding up stores. Two down the street so far. The can ladies who take the cans from the recycling don't come around anymore. People are finally, Finally! obeying the street walking rules. Stay to the right. Which is nice. All it takes is a pandemic for people to finally adhere to social niceties. Maybe I. Weiss will finally call me and apologize. Send me a check. I mean I rigged my fingers to the bone for those jerks. Ten years! And they owe me back wages. Not holding my breath.

I guess Governor Status Cuomo is acting all Presidential at the moment. I don't buy it. I still remember 2018. When he was being primaried by Cynthia Nixon. I still remember him waiting until it was way too late to fix the L Train problem. Pretending it was not in his purview. But suddenly it was politically expedient to get involved. How he opened that bridge that was named after his father, months early, to the possible danger and detriment of everyone who would use it, for political gain. I don't trust that mother fucker. And he should stop fighting with the mayor. If he really means it. And stop wearing those fucking action suits. A douche in a windbreaker doesn't command respect, it just makes you look like a douche wearing a windbreaker.

Made another deep dish pizza. Mushrooms. Bell peppers. Pepperoni. Onions. Made the dough myself. Lots of elbow grease. Professor Curly went to the grocery store. Leather gloves and a bandana over her face. The Grocery Bandit! We'll see how it tastes. I am afraid the dough might be a little salty. Conflicting recipes. Bobby Flay and Wikipedia were my sources. And a couple others. I guess pizza dough is nuanced. Who knew! Made the sauce myself too. Seemed to be missing something. A little sweet.

Still trying to get magic mushrooms. Guess the drug dealers are on lockdown too. The coke dealers probably aren't. Maybe I should change my strategy?

Okay, Professor Curly says it ain't too salty. She opened her bottle of PeriProcseco. Which seems like grapefruit soda mixed with alcohol. Squirt? Is that the name of that soda? If yes, ha!

A friend of ours got in trouble for doing her workout routine in her apartment. Too loud. But jumping jacks? Come on. I thought that was something only kids in middle school and basic training cadets did. They seem useless to me. Just bonk your brain around in your skull for a while. Like jumping on a trampoline as an adult.

Tomorrow I will teach Professor Curly how to use the bathtub to do laundry. Sweatpants. Uggs. Unmentionables. Not sure I am up for the challenge.

I need a haircut. Cut myself shaving today. Bled for two hours. Got light headed. Thought I caught it. Hit the sack. Felt better after. Just joking. About the thinking I caught it. Only a matter of time. Although I did learn today that you shouldn't get shit in your mouth from somebody who has it. It can transfer that way. I also learned, and please don't listen to what I am telling you as medical fact, because it is not, but they say that you feel better right before you get it. Which is an insane thing to tell people! Even if it is true. People are already panicking whenever they feel tired. Whenever they kind of have a weird feeling in their throat. The body panics. It is natural. Now the body has to panic if it is feeling good too! Aye yi yi!

Death is a party that everyone is invited to. It only depends on when you get the invitation.

On a lighter note. I was walking by the window earlier and some guy that was walking by was looking up because he saw me. He pretended like he was looking somewhere else, but there was nowhere else he could have been looking. So he made this really weird unnatural face to hide the fact that he was peeping in the window. Instead of just looking away. It was very cute. I felt for him. Same.

DAY EIGHT

Raining. Supposed to rain all week. I thought today was Tuesday already. Hold yourself together, man!

I feel so lucky that I have a few dollars at the moment. I can't imagine having to make the choice of going to work for some asshole for a couple dollars, or getting sick. Not right now at least. Maybe ten years ago. When my anger was merely self hatred. Now I got self esteem!

You know what they say about the Coronavirus? It took that Contagious to make me dinner. Oh wait, that is a different joke. Something about pro-tein, but anti-body…you know, what with the new self esteem. Oh! now I remember.

You know what they say about the Coronavirus? It will fat-shame you, because it is anti-body.

Or something like that. My brother Jade would be proud. He would also be proud of this invention I invented today to cook potatoes. It is a spatula on a pivot point in the frying pan. At the center. The pivot point. Professor Curly says it needs to be motorized. Now I know why it took that contagious to cook my breakfast.

Enough with the laughs though.

The economy is really fucked. We are at least three weeks behind on this shit. And it doesn't have to be this way. My only hope is that the stock market crashes so hard that the racist anti-poor capitalist assholes in the government, both Republican and Democrat, get scared enough that they understand that things can't go on as they are anymore. I mean, we are in panic mode. Triage. They are deciding, as we speak, about who they should let die in order for the global economy to survive. But what I don't think they understand is that it is already too late. The damage is already done. Nobody is going to be suddenly willing to go back to work to flip hamburgers for $5/hr just so the American economy doesn't crash and burn. Especially at their own risk. To their own health. Nobody trusts the system as it is. Now you are telling me I am on my own, and you need me to get back to work so some rich white guy doesn't lose his shirt? I hate to tell you, We Live In Crisis! Fuck you for ignoring us in the first place! Yeah, maybe your innovation creates jobs, but good luck getting people to work those jobs when all they do is kill us. Especially when your wealth is grown on the backs of our labor. And you don't share it with us.

I am not saying people won't go back to work. People need money to survive. To eat. To care for their families. I am just saying that we were already walking a very fine line. And now that we have fallen off of the wire and there is no safety net, good luck getting us back on that wire. Inertia.

Titanic. We saw the iceberg. We saw the iceberg coming. We did nothing. Now it is too late.

A rant unheeded is a rant denied.

But the government is ready to start printing money as soon as they get the word. There is a shortage of paper bills. Which reminds me, I need to iron the rest of my money. Typical. Too lazy to iron my money. The bank gave me a handout and I don't even treat it seriously. I wonder if the bank thinks I owe them something by using the ATM? Wouldn't surprise me. They are usually assholes whenever I go inside to do some transaction or another. Maybe it is my personality, but I don't think so. I am body-positive! High self-esteem!

Too bad the government doesn't have tests ready so we can figure out how this thing is spreading. Or masks ready so we contain the spread between our caregivers and the sick. Or maybe even some masks for the grocery store workers who have to deal with people all day. Or the mail-people who need to deliver packages of essentials. Or the people at the pharmacy, who are highly trained? Or, I don't know, what the fuck!

We knew this shit was coming! Now all we got is mixed signals and panic? But at least money will be printed. Right when we need it, when inflation renders it useless because 1 percent of the population who is in control of 99 percent of the world couldn't see past the tip of their dick! And even if your dick is twelve inches long, here in three months when 40 million Americans are starving and can't pay rent, and are too scared to go to work, and it is the middle of summer and the electricity bill can't be paid and it is the hottest year on record, I don't know. I understand that the economy is important. I also understand that the economy isn't the stock market. So ignoring 2/3rds of the population/money because 1 percent of the population gets most of their money from this one thing.

It makes me want to go BERSERK!!!!!!!!!1

Medicare for all. Cheaper and more effective. Private choice is an illusion. Your employer decides your choice. And if you are rich enough, you don't need it anyway.

Living wage. Norway has a $20/hr minimum wage as of ten years ago. It is probably $25/hr now. We are fighting for $15/hr. Here and now. In the richest country in the world.

Right to housing. There is no reason a single American shouldn't have an apartment if they want one. Building materials are cheap. We have land.

These three things would create a buffer for what is about to happen. Maybe even keep it from happening. But it is too late. 80 million people die from this pandemic, or 80 million people die from the financial fallout caused by it. It is looking like we might get both.

Get used to the idea of raising a family out of your car.

Drive your car to a body of water. Gas will be hard to find.

Invest in tarps.

Guns.

Shovels.

Rope.

Get to know your local landowners. You will want friends.

If you are a woman, get used to being pregnant.

Kiss your teeth goodbye.

Tools.

Learn how to make leather.

Get used to smells.

Cry now. It won't be tolerated soon.

But these are the easy days. Right now. Make memories. Something to tell your children and your grandchildren. In case you survive.

"It is not like they turned on us, they were never with us in the first place."

Waterby-'The Calm Almonds'

DAY NINE

Warm and sunny. Made tuna salad for lunch. Quesadillas for dinner. Going to have to go to the grocery store tomorrow. Beer and protein. Everywhere joggers. Thinking about making a chicken pot pie. From scratch. Pie crust seems complicated. Need peas. Vegetable shortening. Stocks are up again. Which makes me a little sick to my stomach. Which means that the people in charge of money don't understand what is happening. Which means that we are about to give a bunch of free money to the Oligarchy. Again. Very stupid.

    I keep seeing people carrying groceries in weird mono-color plastic single-use bags. I wonder what that is all about. I think there must be an illegal plastic bag ring. Already. I find it so bizarre that people hold on to something so hard. Something that benefits nobody. Not humans. Not the animals. Not earth. Do grocery store owners really think that people won't keep shopping if they can't use plastic bags? Groceries are kind of essential. What do I know? I got shamed into washing my grocery bag about a month ago. Hard shame. The person that shamed me had to have somebody translate the shame from Spanish to English, so I could understand. What the hell?

Sleep is getting weird. Trying to stay on schedule, but it is not easy. Slept from 8p to 9p yesterday. Got up. Ate a couple tacos. Brushed my teeth. Got in bed. Watched a detective show. Fell asleep from 11p to midnight. Woke up. Drank some water. Was up until 4a. Watching a detective show. Slept from 4a to 930a. Got up. Ate breakfast. Did some stuff. Took a nap from 2p to 3p. Et cetera.

Think I might become soft and pasty. Professor Curly is doing yoga. I may need to go out on long walks. Don't want to be around people. They say you can pour liquid soap in your bathtub and create a makeshift treadmill.

Been talking to my mom more. On the phone. Which is cute. I like my mom. She is nice. She says Wyoming is doing nothing to combat this pandemic. Sadly, I think they will get away with it. But it will be a specious argument. Wyoming has 500,000 people. The size of the state of Colorado. The smallest population in the country. Wyoming. By inhabitants. Vermont is second. In Wyoming you are allotted something like three square miles of space. On average. I think Alaska is the only state that has more. But most people in Alaska live in Anchorage. And come from all over the world.

Getting sick of eating toilet paper. Stole that joke from the internet. Don't know if I made that joke already. My mind is becoming an echo chamber. Professor Curly successfully redirected me from a rant I was making earlier. Don't think I didn't notice. My mom did the same. But she just said she had to go, and hung up. Professor Curly has to live with me. Payback is a mother fucker:

>9a: Lay the groundwork for the rant.
>10a: Cook breakfast. Tie news-related items to rant.
>1p: Make lunch. Add a couple items to rant.
>4p: Make snack. Distract with news story about something I read on Buzzfeed.
>6p: Make dinner. Lull Professor Curly into a false calm as she drinks her PeriProsecco.
>630p: Bring the hammer down!

She won't know what hit her!

"Those fuckers! Three weeks behind the curve! I mean, I saw it coming! And I'm just some asshole who can barely pay the fucking rent! What the fuck do I know! And another thing!"

"Joey, I am tired."

"Go to bed then! Hope you like the world you wake up in!"

"Joey!"

Maybe I will make those beanie-weanies tomorrow. Spice things up.

DAY TEN

Cold and overcast. Macaroni and cheese for lunch. Peanut butter and jelly sandwiches. Potato chips. Apple slices. Sauteed broccoli. Chicken and steak fajitas for dinner. Got in an argument today about In Case of Emergency number. Taught Professor Curly to do bathtub laundry. Went out for a walk after the argument. Came back home. Opened the door. Smacked in the face by a pair of wet panties. Whose are these! They're not mine!

Not mine either. Turns out they might be hers. Doesn't remember. I thought they might be Emily's. They did share a room in Michigan a few weeks ago. Reminded me of the mystery cheese slices on the cutting board last year. Pretty funny. Also, very rude.

CDC: Wash your cigarettes before smoking them.

Gave a guy directions today. Too close for comfort. What the hell, man! You are literally killing me! This is not the time to be lost, and wandering the streets! And the best part is that he had a mask on, but it was pulled down so he could talk to me. Pushing his phone into my face. Felt a little vulnerable after that. Went to the grocery store to celebrate.

Male. Forties. Smoke a few cigarettes a day. A few beers at night. NYC is the hot-spot. CDC says my ass is grass. Make Wall Street pay for my funeral.

Too late to get to Wyoming. Vermont is now closed down. Who is laughing now about all those rants I did about owning a car in the city?

Although I did have this thought today about how money is the only thing that will give you the actual freedom America is supposed to stand for. Which made me sad. I mean, I have always known it to be true, abstractly, but in times like right now, money is the only liberty that exists. I mean, get in your private plane and fly back to Utah, to your compound, and wait it out while the whole world goes up in flames.

Mitt Romney will somehow become the next President of the United States of America.

Could be worse. He does do a pretty good Daniel Day Louis doing Abraham Lincoln impression. Also, he is as far left as you can go on the Republican side when it comes to health care. Also, he looks like Jim Dawson.

Did some bonin' again today. No cops involved. Think it had something to do with getting smacked in the face by a pair of mysterious wet panties, and a particularly erotic rant about Mitt Romney.

The landlord must be quarantined in Boston. Kind of nice. Also, the revolving sublet in the garden apartment seems to have abated. Chalk up another win for the virus.

No work.

No bars.

No bands.

No restaurants.

Sleep.

Writing.

No guilt.

Sucks I can't see my daughter. But we talk every day at noon. During her "soulful" time. She has some pretty funny developments. Imagine being twelve right now. Stuck in your room. Going to school via the internet. Your mom is stuck at home too. Your mom's boyfriend. His nineteen-year-old son in the basement. If it was me, I would have run away from home a week ago. She seems to be handling everything okay though.

Maybe tomorrow Professor Curly will give me a haircut. Supposed to rain.

DAY ELEVEN

Chicken Pot Pudding. Tasty! Gonna need some tweaking though. More liquid. Will hold off on the recipe until perfected. Skillet Pot Pudding? Skillet Joe's Juicy Yum Yum Surprise?

Very sunny today. Jack Ass Governor Status Cuomo made some remarks today that make it seem like there is nothing to worry about and we should stop social distancing. Not that that is what he meant. But have we learned nothing from how the media behaves in the last three years?!

If you take all the headlines and sort them by bullet points. Make a bubble chart. Add some misinformation and politics. That is what people see when they read the news these days. And then you say something like:

"It's something we're working through. The smartest way forward is a modified public health strategy that dovetails and compliments a get back to work strategy. What we did was we closed everything down. Closed everything. If you re-thought that, or had time to analyze it, I don't know that you would say, "quarantine everyone." I don't even know that was the best public health strategy. Young people quarantining with old people was probably not the best public health strategy."

To the Daily Mail that means the President is right and Status Cuomo is an idiot that acted rashly. Let's see you walk that one back. You dick. And now, with new projections coming out that suggest 80,000 people will die if we just do a half-assed response to this pandemic. Now is not the time for re-branding!

Stocks are up again. Looks like someone leaked the conditions of the bailout to Wall Street. SLUSH FUND. Worked perfect twelve years ago! Sure to work this time! If all things are equal. And, if my assessment is correct, we just this year finally pulled out of the last financial crisis. Finally. Which means, think about the future. Take the age you are right now. Add twelve years. That is how old you will be when we recover from this catastrophe. I'll be in my mid-fucking fifties. If I ever thought I would be able to retire or not have to work some dumb-ass job for some greedy prick, those notions are gone now. Enjoy the furlough while you can, kids! The worst is yet to come. Consider this your retirement. Then get back to fucking work!

So many joggers!

I know spring is here. And we are all stuck

inside. But something seems off. Fear of death? I guess I was the only one that got the memo about pouring liquid soap in the bathtub. Treadmills 4EVA.

Been trying to write slower. Milk it. Fine balance though. Being concise is a tool. Oh! someone just got pulled over outside the window. Hold on! Meh. Just giving a parked car a ticket. Fucking cops. Every fucking time. But if I milk it too much, I lose the thread. If I don't milk it enough, I lose the flavor. But I can't go to bed at 9p, that is too early. But if I write for more than three hours I turn parts of my brain on that don't need to be turned on. Plus I will drink too much without noticing. Which makes tomorrow a pain in the ass. Life is complicated, man.

But back to the cops. There is a fine line between strict policing and unjust policing. Like for instance. We have a city shut down due to a pandemic. Traffic itself is affected. Parking is probably not an issue at the moment. There is a no-standing zone along much of Bushwick Avenue from the hours of 4p-7p. But that is because traffic during those hours is usually excessive. Which means that there is essentially an extra lane opened in order to deal with the overflow of traffic. Not now though. People aren't going to work. Not driving. But the police are still handing out parking tickets? I know it is money related. But come on! Give us a fucking break NYC. I think cars should be banned in the city.

I also know that cops are starting to get sick. Can't come in to work. Is this really how we should be using that resource? But what do I know? I'm not the mayor. And this high-stakes game of telephone between the Federal government, the State government, and the City government. I guess we should all expect nothing but chaos.

I think this next time we do Occupy Wall Street, we should all just squat the buildings downtown. Like move into the high rises. Lord knows we won't have apartments at that point. But nobody sees that coming. Not now. Things are just fine. Look over there! Nothing to see here! Plus we gave you $1,200 dollars. You're poor. It is well established that you think that is a lot of money. Eight weeks too late? And wasn't given to the people who actually need it? Come on! Nobody likes the destitute! They smell bad and use up all the free 0.0000001% of money we spend on entitlements! That money belongs to you, taxpayer. So what if we spend fifty cents of every tax dollar making $200 million dollar drones that get blown up in Iran on accident and nearly lead to a third world war. Poor people are stupid. That's why they are poor. Take a look in the mirror!

I know there are things I don't understand. Like

with finance. Money makes money. Lice makes lice. But I do understand that poverty makes poverty. What happens when 20 million people who already have a hard time paying their rent, who can't go to work, or can go to work, but if they go to work they might get so sick that they will die, and if they don't die will end up in an emergency room that they can't pay for?

That is who needs the fucking $1,200 dollars! Not the middle class salary workers who can get by for a month or two. Or the workers who can claim UnEmployment. Those people might be annoyed, but they will be fine in the end. Maybe even grow a brain and vote progressive when they understand the system is actually rigged against them.

What happens when 20 million people suddenly become homeless because they can't pay rent? What happens when that number doubles because the next 20 million people that are barely making it can't do two months of zero income? 40 million homeless Americans. Sound familiar? Shit does not roll uphill.

I mean, it can. If we mobilize. Now.
Stop paying rent.
Go to the bank. Close your account.
Don't return to work.
Don't pay your taxes.
Then we wait.
It is going to suck, but it will be effective. They

need us way more than we need them. It's true. This pandemic will end. But we are sitting on a gold mine here! We have them by the mother fucking balls! All we have to do is act!

And it is just sitting here. Right now. In our laps.

If a 30% loss of GDP is cause for concern, what about 75%? 100%? I don't care anymore. Burn the whole fucking thing down. I joke about the last recession nearly killing me. This one will definitely kill me. I don't have the stomach for it. Twelve more years of getting fucked up the ass by a confederacy of douche-bags?

I don't see it!

The last time the economy crashed we were in a much stronger place. The gig economy didn't exist. People had jobs. This time there is no job to go back to. We don't own anything. There is nothing to fall back on. We all used it up dealing with the last collapse. Our computers are outdated. Everyone owns a crappy phone that they paid too much for. The amount of debt is out of control. Think about it? What do you own that you can sell right now? If you had to. Who the fuck would buy it? Beanie Babies? Wedding rings? Everything we own is crap.

Just sayin.

Buy a tent. Buy a sleeping bag. My guess is that Amazon has a kit for you to buy. But wait until the Coronavirus has subsided first. Because their workers are infected. Like mid-July. Find an empty lot. Post up. Kiss your old life goodbye.

Either that, or we go on a general strike until we get the bare necessities that we need.

Health care.

Living wage.

Housing rights.

$7.5 trillion dollars is now going to this catastrophe that capitalism has created. You still think we can't afford Medicare For All?

On a lighter note, the health care/insurance industry is going to need a lot more money than expected. And very soon. So if you do have health insurance, expect your premiums to skyrocket.

DAY TWELVE

News from the front. Becca swung by. Bloomers! Society aches. It's the same all over. Lonely. Alone.

Cemetery is shut down. Well, not shut down. Closed. To visitors. It seems like people are still dying to get in though.

First roll of toilet paper from the reserves has been deployed. Nineteen left.

Very nice today. Warm even. My daughter came over. Me and her and Professor Curly went for a walk. Followed by a tarot reading. I asked about the economy. Turns out a change is coming.

Fajitas again for dinner. Lunch was ham or turkey sandies. With potato chips. Went to the grocery store. Tortillas are back. Which is nice. My two tries failed. Professor Curly seemed to like them though. Maybe I will try again. Why am I so bad with bread things? I mean, I do cook fast. Maybe that has something to do with it. Patience. I ain't got none.

Stocks are down again. Thank god. Realized what my problem was with the stocks going up when we have over 1,000 deaths in America from this virus. The disconnect. I mean, I know it's obvious, but I am not so certain as to why it is obvious. But it goes like this:

9/11. The world collapsed. Everyone collapsed with it.

Crash of 2008. The world collapsed. Everyone collapsed with it.

Coronavirus. The world collapsed. Sacrifice your grandma for Wall Street.

I am okay with sacrifice. Personal sacrifice. Are you really asking me to put a monetary value on my daughter's grandparents? This is solidarity? It's not funny. All Republicans are going to hell.

Racist liars who hate the poor and only care about money.

What is done is done. I'll let it go. For now.

Bought some chicken backs today. So insane how cheap they are. $2.77 for 2.145 pounds. Professor Curly said, Ew! When I showed them to her. I said, They ain't chicken buttholes. They're just back meat. The same meat from the same chicken, just the back.

I saved at least ten dollars. That is nothing to sniff at. Not in this economy.

But back to Becca. They showed up on their bike. Cute green bucket helmet. I think it was green. Maybe blue. I thought it was a hard hat. HA. Rolled up pants. Socks exposed. Green t-shirt. Mustache. They have been going around the city.

Or, I guess Brooklyn. Seeing people at a distance. Apparently me and Professor Curly ain't the only couple/people thirsty for news from the outside. We have all become lonely dogs. Waiting for the owners to come back home. Barking through the curtains. Then Becca said:

"I'm okay with this. Isolation. Spent three months in a "Home" when I was thirteen. At least they don't do cavity searches. Right?"

"Imagine being a Jew in Nazi Germany." I said.

I tightened the screw on my glasses today. Suddenly my glasses aren't so frustrating. As Tim Murphy would say:

"A pessimist sees the glasses as half-full. An optometrist sees glasses as a way to improve your vision and therefore improve your life."

That old chestnut.

DAY THIRTEEN

Wrote an email to Jeff Bezos last night:

Everyone knows that you will bring the doom to the entire world, but you will sell it back to us cheap. But how about this:

We are on the verge of a new depression. But it doesn't need to be that way. We need money pockets in already depressed inner city areas. A way for new businesses to open. Thrive. With no fear of failing.

Imagine a fountain of youth for the people that need it the most. And that fountain just spits out money. In a way the Government can't provide.

Just sayin.

Turns out his email is jeff@amazon.com. Look it up. Had a bit of a flashback to the old days of the internet before it all turned to trash. What the internet was supposed to be. Equalizer. But whatever. My guess is that he has been waiting for this moment for quite some time. As much as it is hyperbole that Mitt Romney will become President when this is all done. I do think. For certain. That Jeff Bezos will come out of this on top of the world. Although I don't think he is quite prepared for it yet. Hubris, maybe? He is making a killing off of this mayhem. And not because he is betting against the markets. He IS the market. Something tells me he won't take my advice. Although, I think he would be stupid not to. At this point small businesses are not a threat to him anymore.

I have said it before, I will say it again now: He will be the one to give every American $1,000 dollars a month. If people don't have money, they can't buy shit. If they can't buy shit, his business will suffer. I think we will have the first Trillionaire by October. Maybe sooner.

Sadly, this is good news. It was ours to lose. And we lost it. The problem is that he doesn't give a shit about healthcare or human rights.

Chicken Pot Pudding turned out great! Was supposed to call James today and talk about it. I was also supposed to call my brother Charley to talk about flour tortillas. Tomorrow. Didn't feel like being on the phone today. Which is probably rude. And I'm sorry.

You're right. I'm wrong. I'm foolish. And I'm sorry.

But.

Chicken Pot Pudding:
 2 lbs chicken backs
 1/2 lb boneless chicken breast
 canola oil
 2 cups of flour
 salt
 sugar
 pepper
 celery
 carrots
 potatoes
 peas
 onion
 yeast
 butter
 large mixing bowl
 large cast iron skillet
 whisk [or fork]
 warm water
 kettle
 tongs
 bag of tea
 mug
 colander
 cutting board
 knife
 sauce pan
 spoon

Fry chicken backs in oil in skillet. Medium high. Turning often. They will have bones, so they will take some time to cook.

Fill kettle with water. Place on burner. Heat on high until the whistle blows.

Put tea bag in mug. When whistle blows pour some water over tea bag. Fill kettle with more water. Heat again.

When the chicken backs seem cooked through, pour water from kettle on top. Refill kettle. Put on burner. Cook until whistling.

Take off burner. Watch chicken backs boil. When the water reduces add more water.

Do this for a couple of hours.

Add salt as the chicken backs cook. Be careful not to over-salt, but taste the broth as it cooks. Delicate game.

When a couple hours have gone by, remove chicken backs from broth and put into the mixing bowl. Fill with cold water. Peel meat from the bones. Set aside. Put skin and bones back into broth. Also the water used to cool the chicken backs. Cook for another hour.

After an hour has passed, place colander in mixing bowl in sink. Pour broth into colander. Set mixing bowl filled with broth to the side.

Place skillet back on burner.

¥

While all of this is happening, use the time to prepare for the next step.

In my opinion a good recipe is like a mystery novel. You don't really know how the thing will turn out, but you can develop the ingredients like you can develop characters. Use this thought process. Think about things like, Mouth Feel,

Texture, Density, Robustness. All these characters will factor into the Big Reveal in the end.

Peel carrots and potatoes. You can decide how many. Depending on the size of your skillet. I used:

> 4 medium sized potatoes
> 4 medium sized carrots
> 1 large red onion
> 2 cups of peas
> 3 stalks of celery

Peel potatoes and carrots. Cube potatoes. Place in sauce pan. Cover with water. Set to boil.

Chop carrots. Cut celery into 1/2″U's. Cut ends off of onion. Cut in half. Remove outer skins. Slice into 1/4″slices. Set aside.

¥

When the skillet is back up to heat add 2 tablespoons of butter. Fry boneless chicken thighs. Add to chicken backs when cooked through. Let cool.

Turn heat off. Place onions, carrots, celery in skillet. Prepare flour mix.

¥

In mixing bowl combine flour, sugar, salt, and yeast. Add warm water until the mix is as loose, or looser than pancake mix. You want it pretty wet. Like your girlfriend on prom night. Willing, but not throwing up in the bushes at the bonfire/kegger afterwards.

Set aside.

¥

Preheat oven to 450F. Chop chicken and add to skillet.

The potatoes should only cook for 5 minutes once they start boiling. Probably should have told you that before. Drain in colander. Place in skillet. Evenly. Add peas.

Pour liquid broth on top of vegetables and chicken in skillet.

Sprinkle with salt and pepper.

Pour flour mix on top of everything.

Cook for 40 minutes. In middle of oven. Remove from oven.

Let sit for an hour.

Reheat on top of stove. Medium high. Until hot. The liquid will bubble out from under the bread topping.

Cut into wedges and serve in a flat bowl. Scoop liquid with a spoon for added wetness.

Serve with a glass of Guinness on a rainy day.

Enjoy!

Professor Curly claims she really enjoyed this. Said it was better than the last one. By far. Can we trust her taste though? She is with me. What does that say? See what I just did there?

Pretty funny these days. Discipline. She gets up at like 7a, 730a. Works on things. Emails. Etc. I get up around 10a. Cook breakfast. Do stuff. Around 130p make lunch. More stuff. Go for a walk. Come back. Make dinner. Dinner 630p. She goes into the bedroom to "Relax" I retire into the anteroom to "Work" finish around 9p or 10p. Hit the sack. Then repeat.

There was something on the internet today that said: It's a three day work week: Yesterday. Today. Tomorrow.

That was pretty funny.

Shaved today. Would shave everyday if I could, but my beard doesn't grow that fast. Think I want some fried chicken. What that has to do with shaving I don't know. But them's the facts.

I feel like being quarantined is like being pregnant. Everything is just outside of yourself. You have no control of your body. Don't come in here, I farted. What? Normally you are gone at this time of day. Same to ya, Miss Sour Cream. Now I know why we go through that so fast. Where the fuck is the ice cream? Are you serious!

They say that no good art will come out of this Pandemic. I disagree. I think stand-up comedy is about to have a wonderful and well-deserved boom!

Take my wife, please!

DAY FOURTEEN

Two weeks. Plane tickets to Wyoming refunded. Spaghetti and meatballs. Washed my hair. Conditioner. Sunday. Haircut tomorrow. Call James. Call Megan and Charley. Mom.

Professor Curly started writing a new play. It's called, ***How's Joey?*** It's about a couple that is on the brink of a breakup forced to live in isolation as the pandemic ravages the city they love so much. Do they make it? Will the crisis expose their weaknesses? or their strengths? How do we love in a modern world?

Just joking.

I might write that one. Spoiler alert. They don't make it. Turns out stealing that last bite of ice cream was the last straw. Just joking. I really don't care for ice cream. Well, most of the time. And right now, I couldn't care less.

Been microdosing the mushrooms the last couple days. So far so good. But only been eating the stems. A little intrigued as to what will happen when I start eating the caps. Things might get a little groovy around here!

We are in a prison of our own minds. Already. The quarantine doesn't change that, man. The guitar solo just kicked in. Give me a second.

Fucking internet. Buzz kill. Get kicked off like twenty times a day. Now. I would go solo, but I ain't got one of those cords. The land line ones.

In other news. I read this article about this group of guys that have been living on an island in Maine for the last month. Doing construction work. Apparently the locals got suspicious and cut down a tree to block them from going out because they had New Jersey plates. On their truck. Pointed guns at them. And what started the altercation is that the internet was down, so one of the guys went out to check out what happened. Unclear if the local vigilantes cut the internet wires or not, but their service was interrupted.

I expect to see more articles like this. Very soon. Florida is already stopping people from coming in with New York and New Jersey plates. The same fuckers who refused to shut down Spring Break! are now not letting liberal dip shits in because they might be infected. The same fuckers who just infected the entire fucking country so they could save their local economy! My god! I hope we have long memories. Because this shit is not okay. Ron DeSantis should be in fucking jail. Right now.

This is not a theoretical. This is happening.

Right now. And all those models that suggest we are three weeks behind the curve are now saying we are eight weeks behind the curve. All the money in the fucking world will not make up for that. Drop your socks and grab your cocks.

This is just the beginning.

And if we are smart. Smart enough. The worst thing will happen is that we will be really bored for three or four weeks. But being smart is not in the "American" purview. Everything we hold dear needs to be taken from our cold dead hands. Live free or die. Et cetera. Make sure your elderly neighbors are doing okay. Get them groceries. Walk their dogs.

Hunker. Get to know your grocer. I tried today. It did not go well. Me and the Red Headed Annie Oakley went out to get baking goods and beer. Gloved and face bandana'd. I asked the check out guy how things were going, how he was doing, if they needed any help. He told me I could pick up an application from the manager if I wanted a job. Not my point. But okay.

I don't blame him. He is a young, gay, Latinx guy who works at a grocery store in Brooklyn. Owned by Latinx. He already has it pretty fucking hard. The look in his eyes, above his mask, said:

"Dude, I don't fucking know. I need this job. I smoke as much weed as I can before I come to work. And now we have this Coronavirus nonsense. Go bug somebody who gives a shit."

So it is. I will try again in a few days. See if they need help. I assumed they were overwhelmed, but maybe not. I did get bag-shamed that one time. Maybe they run a clean ship? The loading dock says otherwise. But who am I to note the obvious? Inspector Dumb Shit?

New York Post: White Guy In His Forties Man-Splains Coronavirus To Latin Grocery Store In Brooklyn. Gets Shot. Community Tight-Lipped.

DAY FIFTEEN

How successful is American Capitalism if it has to be bailed out by American Socialism every ten years? Read that today, somewhere. Very frustrating thought. I know I should stop being frustrated by the current events. It has always been like this. But the problem I am having is this:

Either bend over and take it up the ass, or fight back.

Not that taking it up the ass is entirely unpleasurable. The idiom is both sexist and homophobic. Not to mention it suggests victim shaming, but I am trying to convey a certain submissiveness.

It is crazy that the current administration has left us so vulnerable to this global pandemic. It is also very crazy that the solution is to give trillions of dollars to businesses and structural inequities that have been encouraging this vulnerability in the first place.

The tension on the street in Brooklyn, in my neighborhood, right now, is untenable. It is just the beginning. Shit is going to get very ugly. There is no police. Which is fine by me, but things are already getting lawless. Cars started running red lights. Driving 50-60 mph down the road. Thank god all the children are inside. Screaming matches on the sidewalk. I made sure the locks on the doors work today. Checked out the hatch that leads to the roof. Am thinking of throwing an emergency kit together for when me and Professor Curly have to escape through the hatch when mobs of hungry and angry people can't take the injustice anymore and start looting. And they will have every right to.

The one thing, the one fucking job that the Government is supposed to do, above all else, is to protect the people. And they are failing. Have failed.

Rent is due in two days. And by dumb luck I am in a good position. I really have no idea what I would do if this was just one year ago. Even worse if it was two. Or even earlier last fall. I would be fucked.

But whatever, no one wants to hear a money rant right now.

Saw somebody loaded onto an ambulance today. Not sure if they were dead or alive. They looked pretty dead. People are wearing masks while driving their cars. No haircut. Didn't call my mom. Or James. Or Charley and Megan. Emotional burnout. Couldn't sleep last night.

Been meaning to call Scott and ask him about UnEmployment stuff. I don't need money now, but should I try and get some while I can? Is that a stupid panic thing that will make things worse in the long run? At the moment I can only assume the $16,000 dollars I was gonna make this summer is no longer going to happen. Can I even collect UnEmployment? If I wait to collect, does that mean I am losing out on thousands of dollars I will need in the future?

The system is fucked. Sociopaths will inherit the earth. Am I stupid if I don't act like a sociopath right now?

The Saudis will buy billions of dollars of guns from us, if we don't sell them the guns, somebody else will, I would be stupid not to take their money.

Is that what the world is coming to? Do I want to be part of that reasoning? There was a moment after 9/11 when I was talking with my friend Iver about NYC being hit with a nuclear bomb and he said: I don't think we should leave. Even if we do get blown up with a nuclear bomb, I don't think I would want to live in a world where New York is blown up by a nuclear bomb. Or something to that effect. And I agree. Plus I think it would be pretty cool to die that way. Vaporized. Although the reality is that it would be the fallout that would kill you. Which would really suck. Radiation poisoning and thirst. I can't think of a worse way to die.

I don't know. I don't fucking know. My friend Luke sent me this poem today. About this guy watching the world go by. Smoking cigarettes and being grumpy. How everything he has ever done is collected in his body and it is okay to do nothing at a certain point. Because, fuck it. I did my best. But I don't know if I have done my best yet! I don't feel like I have! There is an itch back there, in the back of my head that I haven't scratched yet!

But who knows. Maybe that is by design. Why we keep coming back. Making babies. Maybe that is why Siddhartha did all that naked wrestling on top of those ant hills. Just to scratch that fucking itch.

I don't know. Poetry is weird. Every time I write some I feel stupid. But a good rant though!

Professor Curly and me and her sister are thinking about starting a podcast. The Rant. Which is just me and her sister yelling at her for an hour about the same stupid shit that we agree on and think that Professor Curly doesn't have all the information on. But what is good about it is the visual. It will be Professor Curly in the middle. Plugging her ears. While me and her sister are in profile on either side screaming.

The world needs more podcasts.

Leftovers all day. Guess I will go to the grocery store tomorrow. Need more beer. Don't know where it all goes. Think Professor Curly secretly has a drinking problem. Half of me hopes the grocery stores will run out of beer. The other half of me says, Man! Pull your shit together! Thirty more days of isolation! At least! But I am disciplined. 6p-9p. Drink beer. Any more than that is just trouble. Any less than that would be trouble too. My brain is like a train whistle. If I don't blow it off every now and again, the cows won't get off the tracks. And this train that I am the conductor of does not have a cattle catcher. It is weak. And it will derail.

But enough about my love life. Speaking of which. Did some bonin' today. Bj by the window. UPS guy caught us this time. Is this becoming a thing? Blow jobs by the window while men in uniform lurk outside? I think it is coincidence. That is where Professor Curly does her business. I do mine in the kitchen. But it has happened twice now. The first time was a police officer. But how many places are there to have sex in any given apartment? In ours? The floors. Maybe the oven top. We don't have enough counter space. I am strong, but wall sex is unlikely. We have a lot of paintings. That leaves the couch and the bed. So by process of elimination, blow jobs by the window! QED

But maybe Professor Curly gets off on giving blow jobs by the window while men in uniform lurk outside? Possibly watching? She's dirty.

Maybe that is why she secretly drinks beer all day. Keeping her nerve up. So she is ready to get her rocks off when the right time comes. Damn! That girl is a dirty bird!

DAY SIXTEEN

Beanies. Weanies. Professor Curly got it again. Although she hasn't been outside in a couple of days. Shows no signs. But she is tired. God speed, PC!

Talked to my sister Amy today. Which was nice. Been a while. Wyoming seems to be acting pretty dumb. Not surprising. Biggest percentage voted for the Orange Douche in 2016. By state. Like 94%. Don't quote me on that. But something big like that. If anyone should be worried it is them. Not because they might get infected. The risk is pretty low. But because if they do get sick: there are plenty of beds. But almost no ventilators. Half the towns don't even have hospitals. Those helicopter flights from wherever, Wyoming to Denver, or Billings, or Salt Lake are really fucking expensive. And for a state that doesn't believe in health insurance unless you can afford it and where paying back personal debt is a moral imperative...[I repeat]...[double ellipsis] that is a life ruining event.

Read an article today that suggested Andrew Cuomo has pierced nipples. There was a photograph. Wish that was true. I would like him more. But I think he just has big nips with pimply things and hairs. Which doesn't make me like him more.

Professor Curly made oatmeal cookies today. Maybe that is why she is tired. She used a lot of elbow grease. Cookies taste great! Had to freeze half the batter. She made fifteen cookies. At three cookies a day, that is enough cookies for a week of lunches [work week] but there was enough batter left over for at least fifteen more. I'm not complaining. That is just a lot of cookies!

Stocks are down again. Ending the worst quarter since 2008. Which is good. No way to spin that shit. Coronavirus or not. The rich must be losing their shit. We are all fucked. But now they are fucked too. It's official.

And it will only get worse. NYC, which has taken this seriously since the very beginning, is projected to peak out in a couple weeks and should be fine by the end of April. But so what? We can maybe open businesses again on a local scale by then, but so what? The rest of America, aside from Washington and California, are just now getting their shit together. Which means that they won't be out of the danger zone until the end of June. Earliest. Probably the end of July. And tourism is a huge part of our economy. I don't expect people to flock to the city just because we are ahead of the curve. Not when more than half of the country is still on lock down. Imagine buying a ticket to Rome right now just because flights are cheap. For July. Not going to happen. Not to mention that they wouldn't let you fly there anyway. Because Americans are idiots.

But money! The Economy! he bellowed.

Drop out! What was the phrase from the 60's? Turn on, tune in, drop out? We have the fucking numbers. Get off of Facebook. Gmail. Get an AOL account. Mindspring. I don't know, anything! Just shift the fucking numbers! Rent strike! Tax strike! Don't pay your credit card bills. Your student loans. Burn the thing down! You don't owe these fuckers anything! Debt is not a moral thing. Wake up! You are being gaslit! Your car payment. They can come for some of us, but they can't come for all of us. And when they realize that they should have treated us better, it will be too late. Society is already in tatters. This mayhem has fallen directly into our laps! Cancel Netflix. Read a fucking book!

Write a book, instead. Eat beans and corn tortillas for a month! Sit around and do nothing. I don't know, talk to the person you love instead of ranting at them while they get ready for their video conference.

We will be just fine. We always have been. It is the financial institutions that will not be fine. We should all just sit here. Waiting. And when they beg us to go back to work, we should all speak in our loudest and most bitter voices, and yell, FUCK YOU!!!!!!!!!!!

You caused this. You should pay for this. It didn't need to be this way. But your greed and malfeasance led to your demise. Fuck you. Fuck all that you stand for. Fuck you. I am a human, and as a human, I deserve respect. Fuck You.

DAY SEVENTEEN

Trouble in paradise. Three days since Professor Curly has been outside. She is getting weird. I am getting weird too. My dreams are now just processing emails I send. Phone calls. Aside from Professor Curly I haven't seen anyone I know for four days now. I think since Sunday. Today is Thursday. I think. I did do a pretty funny April Fool's joke. We were supposed to fly into Cody, Wyoming today. Me and Professor Curly. We called Charley and Megan today. The first thing I said when they picked up the phone was, Hey! We're in Cody! Where the hell are you guys? Megan said, What! Are you serious! I said, April Fool's!

I guess you had to be there. But it was pretty good. Topical.

Made a loaf of bread. Success. Beanies and Weanies again for dinner. With fresh buttered bread. Not bad. Don't know why my body likes hot dogs. But my body likes hot dogs. Who am I to judge.

Sandwiches for lunch. Zesty mustard spread and bacon bits. Not Baco-Bits. Do they still make those? Pretty smart idea. Been putting any half-used vegetables in the empty pickle jar with pickle juice. Maybe I already mentioned that. But that is a good idea too. This is not the time to throw away unwanted waste. Waste not want not. Ignorance is bliss. A penny for your earning is early to rise. Wealthy and early found in bed.

A wealthy penny is found in the morning.

Stocks are down again. This time pretty bad. Whatever. All those poor billionaires. I guess when they all promised to donate half their wealth to fighting global poverty and didn't invest like they said they would. Well, whoops. That investment would be paying off right about now. How about instead you just lose half your wealth anyway. You greedy fucks. Oh, and it is just the beginning. Get ready to eat dirt, you fucks.

Still traffic on Bushwick Avenue. Which confuses me. Where are all these people going? Or coming from? Whenever the lights change there is something like fifty cars going either direction. All day long. It is baffling. Do people just live a vastly different life than I do? They must. But where? I have been stuck at home for over two weeks now. I assume they are coming or going to work. But where? Nothing is open. Maybe they are just driving around because they have nothing to do. Gas is cheap. I assume. Oil prices are rock bottom.

The wells are all filled up. Nobody is buying. Isn't that how capitalism works? Supply/Demand?

Maybe it is anti-American to not drive around. Stink up the place. Kill a couple dolphins on your daily rounds. Melt an iceberg for Uncle Sam. America is fucked. Nobody is going to take us seriously again for at least twenty years. If not longer. And if we somehow get this Orange Douche for four more years. America will not exist anymore. They will take Obama, Hillary and Nancy out back on the first day and shoot them. Make political parties illegal. Then brag about bringing the country together under one party. I hope you understand this.

They say that I eliminated the Democratic party. I say no, I did not eliminate the Democratic party, I eliminated all the parties! There will be no need for a revolution for one thousand years!

But by then we will be starving on the streets and won't care one way or the other. Half of us will be glad to be in jail. At least we get food. And a warm place to sleep. The other half will sign the loyalty oath. But who am I to judge.

Just a warning though. Think back to all the emails you have sent in the last three years. Maybe delete them now. Not that that will make a difference. But it will buy you some time. And starting today, only speak highly of the Government. It is your only way out.

I am not coming with you. But just a heads up.

Because it was them! They caused this! It doesn't need to be this way. We, as a people, don't need to be dragged into the dirt with the capitalist gaslight mantra that says, You are born this way! You should live this way! You should die this way! You are stupid!

We need so little!

A place to live. A wage to earn. A doctor to go to. Then leave us the fuck alone!

I read something today about how the new iPhone was coming out. I thought it was a joke. But it is not a joke. I suppose we should make Cocaine Inc. public. So we can trade on that too. Lord knows illegal drug futures are higher than ever. A depressed economy needs a distraction. Invest in booze as well. And hand guns.

Suicide Incorporated.

DAY EIGHTEEN

An ambulance just showed up on the corner. I watched the EMTs put all their safety gear on before they went inside. I suppose that is protocol now. Three buildings down. Can't get much closer. Is it a question of If, still? Or is it a question of When? Professor Curly thinks we should go get supplies for five days tomorrow and not leave the apartment. I agree. Sounds brutal, but I agree.

Supposed to have a phone interview with K2 tomorrow. They are the news station in Casper, Wyoming. I did an interview with them last summer. When **Killing The Math 2** came out. I guess the idea is to talk about what it's like out here. I will call Brian when I am done writing this.

The coffee shop across the street is still open. That bugs me. But in their defense, they bugged me long before this pandemic. Professor Curly seems to find them entertaining. And they did hold that package for me that one time. I just don't think they need to be open. Not right now. It is kind of serious. But who knows, maybe they are watching the person get wheeled off into an ambulance right now. Directly across the street from them. Could have a change of mind.

Sandwiches for lunch. This time with freshly homemade bread. I started putting any leftover chunks of onion, or jalapeño or whatever vegetable in the jar that has no pickles, but has pickle juice. Nice little relish is brewing. I wonder what would happen if you put little chunks of cheese in there? Probably pretty tasty!

Dreamed about stealing a honeycomb from a beehive last night. Did some research on the meaning. Not good. But funny:

Stealing honey in a dream is a sign of unhappiness in the family and making distance with them.

A little on the nose, Internet, don't you think? Whatever happened to subtlety?

Well, good news. I suppose. They didn't wheel anyone off into the ambulance. Bad news is that somebody was sick enough to call the ambulance. Wish them the best. Feel bad I don't know my neighbors better. But this block is so hard. Very busy. And there seems to be a lot of turnover. So people are naturally suspect of anyone new. I also have one of those personalities that suggests you should probably avoid me. Which doesn't help. But I think I am nice. I try to be good.

Mushrooms are gone. My microdosing days are over. Too bad. But like Scott says, Microdose with the mushrooms you have, not with the mushrooms you want. So true. Guess I am back to microdosing beer again. Yuck. God yeet-eth and god yoink-eth away.

Stocks are up. Even though the UnEmployment just jumped to Ten Million. They say it has something to do with oil. Cute.

Need to do laundry again. All my shirts are too small. My back-up shirts. From before I got middle-aged. Nothing fits right. And now I got all this inactivity. The boulder is getting harder to push up the hill. My socks fit just fine though. Why is that? My poor turtle-necks.

One day. When this is all over. I am going to move to Wyoming. Or Vermont. Iron my money there. Write a novel so long you have to read it on a Rolodex. And it will be so fucking boring that they will have to teach it in college classes for one hundred years. And I can laugh my ass off all the way to my grave. And my grave stone will be that Jack-Ass prank where you have to read the fine print and when you get closer a boxing glove on a spring will punch you in the face.

But for now. Life is boring. But I am making good boring memories to put in my Rolodex novel for later. Suck it.

DAY NINETEEN

Found a brand new pair of pants in the closet. Professor Curly says they look like Huskies. They rub on my chubby places though. Took a nap. Did some bed bonin'. Made another bread loaf. And a vegetable soup. Did my laundry in the bathtub. Made a mask out of an old pair of my daughter's pajama bottoms. From when she was like six. Mixed emotions. On one hand, they were very cute and reminded me of when she was six. On the other hand, it was creepy to cut a pair of children's pajamas up to make a pandemic mask. Pink. With little flowers.

The K2 interview is on hold until next week. It will take place with one of the reporters though. Instead of Billy, the morning talking head.

Cold and rainy. The daily walks are getting depressing. People just stopped picking up their dog shit. Everything feels bleak. Stocks are down again. Yesterday, stocks, "Soared" on news of an agreement between the Saudi's and the Russians, about gas. Today, stocks, "Down" amid dismal jobs numbers. Funny thing is that the numbers are nearly the same. So what is it? Are they, "Up" yesterday, or did they, "Plummet" today? So much horse-shit these days. Trying my hardest not to go into a financial rant. But I heard all this nonsense today from "Experts" about what is happening with the economy, and it is becoming very apparent that they don't know shit, none of them, and they are just making it all up as they go along. Who can blame them though? I have plenty of ideas and opinions about this subject, just nobody asks me what I think. And you know what I think about that?

It stinks.

I mean, we are fucked. And until they can figure out how to get money into the hands of the people who actually need it, the people who make the economy run, the workers and renters and the barkeeps and the wait staff and the babysitters and the guy that collects all the debris on the job sites, then they are fucked too. I'll leave it at that. For now.

Didn't manage to go to the grocery store. Gets harder each time. It is a pretty serious game of roulette. A month ago I figured I would just get it and it would suck, but I would be all right in the end. Now I'm not so sure. The article about how you are more likely to die if you smoke is making the rounds again. But in that same article it says that if you smoke you are less likely to get the thing in the first place. Should I smoke more? Smoke less? Am I fucked either way? But then they say that there is a possibility I already have it. And I don't even know it. But then they say only the elderly and compromised people die from it. Then they say that anyone middle aged will die from it. Then I read that some guy that is 101 got it and is just fine. Then they say that men are more at risk of dying. Then they say a baby just died from it.

I know I read too much news. But come on people! Get the message straight!

It used to be you would read the New York Times, the NY Post, the NY Daily News, and the Washington Post, and somewhere in between you the truth would lie. But now we got:

The NY Times is terrified of the Orange Douche for some reason

The NY Post is too racist to read

The NY Daily News is just USA Today mixed with AP news and watered down with a glass of water

The Washington Post is who the hell knows what? Hilary 2.0?

Speaking of which. I had a thought today. Why the Right is so afraid of Biden. The Southern Strategy. What they have been using since Nixon. They know the elderly white vote will be 50/50 Republican/Democrat. So all they really need to do is to get a small percentage of the black vote. And since everyone else will be too demoralized and disillusioned to vote, that is all that they would need to win. But Biden is beating them at their own game! And since the DNC is using the same strategy, they know this too! Too bad the fuckers won't vet the fucker before the election. Lord knows the RNC will have no problem dragging his ass through the mud when the time comes. And who cares that the Orange Douche voters will walk through fire to vote for him, and nobody really gives a shit about Biden – it is all the same to them. I suggest you invest in Biden 2020 Voting Nose Plugs. We will need them like hot cakes.

Professor Curly bought me some slippers. They are very comfy. Maybe that is where I finally get it from. You let your guard down for one second!

"The biggest danger to personal survival: A passive outlook, and a desire for comfort."

-Handbook for the Airborne Rangers

I really want to go on a rant about finance. But I won't. I had an epiphany today that needs to be developed. But damn! It is good. Just ask yourself this one question:

What happens when America defaults on Chinese loans?

I tried to watch **Red Dawn** the other day. Does not hold up. I mean, maybe we would willingly die to fight communism, I really doubt it, but okay, maybe, thirty years ago, but how many Americans would be willing to die to pay back a Chinese loan?

Luckily we have a government that has been developing Passive-Nukes. Micro-Nukes? Local-Nukes? Whatever they are called. The ones that will blow up the Laramie, Wyomings of the world. However, that won't really matter once the dollar collapses against the kroner because we didn't take this pandemic seriously and all of our money is useless. The right wing tears the Europe Union apart. And guess what? China and Russia will be just fine. Not because they are smarter. Just because Democracy will be dead. Jeff Bezos will be king of the world. The Orange Douche will fly Air Force One to Moscow and become Putin's lap-dog.

It will be every state for itself at that point.

But don't conflate this with the Economic Theory I am working on!

This is not a rant!

Stay gold, Ponyboy!

DAY TWENTY

Weekend! Finally. Taco night. Crunchy Benders, as Tim Murphy would call them. Flavor Town. French toast for breakfast. Professor Curly had to go to the grocery this morning for bacon. Sausage too. I went in the afternoon for beer and taco stuff. Tried once again to ask how the cashier was holding up. Nothing doing. Either they are pissed. Or don't care. Or are sick of people being concerned about them. Will never know. Everyone seems unwilling to talk about it. Kind of reminded me of going through a toll booth on the interstate. All waiting and business. People paranoid about getting cut in front of. Clueless people trying to cut in line. People with only a few items trying to cut in line too. Maybe they didn't get the memo. I don't know if running to the store to get a bottle of juice and package of chewing gum counts as essential movement. But the people that are doing that are also the same people who aren't wearing gloves or a mask.

I don't know. Maybe it is like going through

airport security too. But without somebody telling you where to go. Which gives me conflicting feelings. On one hand, we need order right now. The chaos is palpable. On the other hand, I don't really want some authoritarian goon with a sudden and uneven power barking orders at me when I am just trying to stock up on supplies. Whatever. I just hope they have a plan when food starts getting scarce. When people start getting hungry but don't have any money. When things have a propensity for violence.

Nice out today. Warm. Sunny. Streets are filled with idiots. No stock trading.

Watched my friend Jack's mask video on-line today. Missed the live stream. But the masks look amazing. He keeps trying to lure me to Williamsburg. I don't know. I am nervous as fuck about going anywhere at the moment. But it would be nice to blow some steam off. But it is an hour and fifteen minute walk. Through Butthole Town. Meaning Williamsburg. But I can assume his studio is clean. Everyone is out of town. But the timing. Not so good.

My daughter has Spring Break! next Wednesday. They cancelled it, but then they un-cancelled it. Which I guess is a good idea. I mean the teachers must be out of their minds right now. However, school at the moment is six hours of something to do. For both parties. The kids and the teachers. But who the fuck am I to judge. I ain't done shit for nearly three weeks now. I could use a vacation myself. But my daughter just got this video game thing in the mail. Animal Crossing. That is the game. The hand held device is called like, I don't know, Gameboy For 20 Years Later And New Games, kind of. Which I think will be good for her. For these times. Tetris. Escape From Kamp Krusty. Metroid. I would probably hang myself from boredom if I was fwelve. She also has a cat. And her own room. And no stupid brothers to compete with all the time. When I was her age during a pandemic all me and my four brothers had to play with was a pubic hair we found in the bathroom and a pillow with an unidentifiable smell.

Shaved today. Mirrors, man. Don't get me wrong. I ran out of mushrooms, so this isn't ersatz philosophical projection. I just. I mean, I can see the future. And it isn't pretty. It's nice to have a mirror to shave in, but I am not sure we need so many of them. The only thing they do is make you feel bad. You know? It is either, suspension of disbelief, where you say to yourself, Okay, not yet. You still have a few good years. Or, Well, you did the best that you could with the things you were given. Maybe it is time to throw in the towel. And then you find yourself pulling hair clusters from your chin in the harsh afternoon light thinking, Damn, I should really go to the dentist. And then you smile like an antelope and think about all the dead animals you have seen in your life with really dirty teeth. Then you feel totally and horribly alone. Because nothing you do, nothing you change in your life, will prevent the inevitable thing that connects you to all living beings. Which is death. That you, yourself, will die.

Jack says they are starting to board up businesses on Bedford Avenue. He thinks that it has violent indications. [This is my interpretation from a phone call, fyi. Don't sue me Jack for defamation!] That we are preparing for rioting and looting. Which, I think, is probably true. Things will start to get very bad, very soon. But I take a more pragmatic approach. Most businesses have big windows. If you can't be at your business all the time, it is likely that somebody will break your window. Drunks are always lurking around. Half angry. And real clever. Brick clever. And if you don't go to your business everyday, you should take measures to prevent people from destroying it. But at the same time, we live in a city. Crime is a result of a disparity of income and a disparity of resources. And Bedford Avenue is the epitome of that. If I had a business on Bedford Avenue right now, I would not board up my windows, I would rent a truck and remove all of my inventory and place it in a shipping container in Connecticut. But then I wouldn't ever open a business on Bedford Avenue. Not because it is a bad business investment, but because it would be morally wrong to. But who am I to judge? Poor neighborhoods should be exploited. Poor people are stupid. If they weren't stupid, they wouldn't be poor.

I don't know. This is all just a great big bummer. I should end on a positive note. This is from, ***A Crack-Up At The Race Riots***, by Harmony Korine:

"My girlfriend entered a good-lookin' legs contest. She lost out to the microphone stand."

Oh no, you didn't.

DAY TWENTY-ONE

Three weeks! Celebrated with Oxtail and Rice Pilaf. Frozen spinach. Flour tortillas. I tried again. This time using my brother Charley's recipe. Same result. Starting to think the problem is the flour itself. I wonder if I can maybe toast it before I use it. They just taste so raw. Raw Dog Torts: Big Floppy Saltine Crackers. I don't know. Maybe I am just too sensitive. I got a sensitive tongue. Just ask Professor Curly's bean.

Speaking of wet beans, I got nothing. Everything is racist. I was going to go for the Co-ed joke about riding an [writing an] Ese [pronounced Essay] that my brother Kevin told me, who is Mexican, mind you, but it always falls flat. So, good job, Political Correctness, you ruined my life once again.

Status Cuomo is at it again. Declaring the worst is over. Apparently the numbers of deaths in New York dropped a little. Rather than say something like, We saw a drop in numbers today, which is a good sign, but we should wait and see if it keeps going down. He instead said, "The apex could be a plateau. And we could be on that plateau now." The fucking douche. At the same time the Mayor of New York is begging for help. And the people of New York are looking for any reason, Any Reason, to not have to stay inside anymore. Combine that with the Orange Douche insisting that we open up business regardless of the death toll. Combine that with the corporate media screaming, We "Will" hit the apex in eleven days. For the first time in three weeks I had the feeling that it is time to abandon ship, damn the consequences. Because if the Governor of New York and the President are thinking the same thing, we are all fucked. It is the worst of all worlds.

Eat your shit cake and have your diarrhea soup too.

Fuck your politics. Both of you.

First of all, we can't hit the apex in eleven days. There is zero evidence of that. There is a projection of that, but that would mean we had competent leadership that didn't send out mixed messages, combined with American citizens taking the threat seriously. I mean, there are still something like ten states that are doing virtually nothing to combat this. So instead of just shutting everything down for two weeks and being done with this, it's going to bounce around for months and months and make it impossible to go back to work.

Second of all, there is nothing, literally nothing, that is stopping this from spreading. Aside from staying home and washing your hands and wearing gloves and a mask when you go out to get groceries. And staying away from other people. The malaria cure our Orange Douche is selling on the television just kills people and makes things worse for lupus sufferers. Because they can't get access. The Lupus sufferers. All the other "Cures" are just normal nonsense about being healthy in the first place. Vitamin C. Zinc. Good diet and exercise. Yes, being healthy is a good idea, but it is not a "Cure."

Third of all, so what if we open New York up again. It will be months before the country will be open. Mostly because we didn't collectively take this seriously in the first place. Nationalism breeds chaos. Boris Johnson just got taken to the hospital because of this pandemic. If he dies. I mean, if the fucking Prime Minister of England dies of this virus, I will do a fucking dance. Just desserts.

Fourth of all, the Boris Johnson of America, the Orange Douche, telling us to go back to work. I mean, and I don't think I mean just me, I think, I mean, to be the collective, all of us, Colgate, unless that fucker stands behind that fucking podium in the fucking Rose Garden, the Orange Douche, and pulls a pistol from his pocket and says, I am willing to die for all of America to get back to work, and blows his head off on live TV, I think we should stay at home. I will not die for him. I will not die for Wall Street.

Remember when the American death toll from this was supposed to be 6,000? If we did everything right? Now it is nearly half of that every single day? Florida hiding its numbers to give the President a better number? I mean, I know that America was born a capitalistic endeavor. That white, slave-owning, land-lording males, who didn't want to pay taxes, created this country. I am done. I want it to stop. This administration is a cancer on society. And it needs to end.

When Joe Biden has a stroke next month and can't be the front runner anymore, I think we should nominate the progressive I had in a dream. It wasn't Bernie. It was a woman in her forties. She had a cool black outfit. United us all. Be On The Lookout.

But not Status Cuomo, nor his stupid brother. Those dudes are douches.

Bernie though. He would rip the Orange Douche's marbles to shreds.

Bernie 2020

DAY TWENTY-TWO

Okay. So Boris Johnson is now in the ICU. I feel a little bit bad for wishing death upon him. I still think he is a horrible piece of shit that has no business being the Prime Minister of England, and maybe, just maybe, if he survives, he will reconsider de-funding the public health care system in England. I doubt it, but good faith. I guess. On a lighter note, the Orange Douche just blew his brains out on live TV. Just joking.

Speaking of horrible pieces of shit. The fucking ice cream truck just came around. The fucking sadistic bastard. Yeah, I know, trying times, no money coming in, et cetera, but fuck you! Health risks aside, those poor, poor children. Stuck inside. No outlet. Nothing to do all day. And this fucker comes cruising by. His repugnant tune, blaring. I mean. Children's faces plastered to the window. Memories of summer and ice cream. A special place in hell. A special place in hell.

Pizza night! Pepperoni and onion. Thin crust. For a size queen like Professor Curly, she doesn't like the Deep Dish. What is that all about? Sauteed broccoli on the side. Guinness to snorkel. I call the dinner Chunks Delight. She thinks she is so fancy. Fat shame me in a dream, she better wake up and apologize.

Speaking of new developments, I came up with an idea for a murder-mystery. A woman gets murdered during a pandemic. But because of government mandated social distancing measures, nobody notices. But, also, the guy that kills her has a daily web-log that involves her, so he is able to pretend that she is still around and nobody gets suspicious. But, also, he has a whole month to deal with her dead body. Which is nice because it gives him something to do. I think I will call it, ***How's Tina?***

Professor Curly just yelled from the other room, That dinner we just had tonight at 6:32p on Monday, April 6th, was delicious! Thanks Joey!

What a weirdo. Am I right? I guess I will write this screed and go sleep in the bed with her all night and then get up in the morning tomorrow and spend the day with her again. And then the next day too. And also all the other days we are in lockdown. What's that? Coming! I gotta go. She needs a glass of water. I should go.

I'm back! Where was I?

My brother Charley thinks I should maybe fry the tortillas in butter before I serve them. Which I am not against. The problem though is not that they aren't tasty enough. The taste is fine. Although bland and unsatisfying. The problem is that they are not what I want to make. Maybe I have wimpy hands. Or wimpy elbows. My first dishwashing job, when I was a teenager, was at this place called The Office. And, Mikell, the owner, my boss, always had me make the hamburger patties for the night because I was the best at it. Because I had such a tender touch. Well, at least that is what she would tell me every time she cornered me in the walk-in cooler asking me to feel her up. Just joking. She was very sweet. I really am just joking. Not about being sweet. Wonderful woman. Human. Wonderful human. She never molested me. Nor did she have me molest her. But I also did have the softest elbows in town, hands down, for many, many years. Ask Jacob. He knows. He told me multiple times in the walk-in closet at the Old Towne Tavern in Ballard, Seattle. Just joking. The Old Towne never had a walk-in cooler.

I don't know. Maybe I just need to treat the batter harsher. Really rub it out. I just love the flour tortillas you get from the store. It is not the same with the corn tortillas. Fresh-made corn tortillas are by far superior. Ask Scott. He showed me how to use the corn tortilla press in the chicken coop for some reason. Said it was our secret. Whatever that means. But the tortillas we made in the chicken coop were very satisfying. He took pictures. Where those pictures went, I couldn't tell you. But they are out there. Somewhere.

Seven Layer Tuna [Eight, if you Remember About the Nuts]
   small frying pan
   large bowl
   spoon
   paper towel
   bread [four slices]
   one can of tuna [in water]
   four baby carrots [Or one regular carrot. I tried to explain to Professor Curly that baby carrots are just regular carrots whittled down. She doesn't care. Choose your battles.]
   part of an onion [I used white onion today. It was mild. I guess it depends on whether you like lots of onion flavor or not. But I am starting to come around to white onions. They have more meat. And the same flavor as all onions. Which is onion flavor. Jacob can't stand onions. They remind him of rats' tails. I also had a roommate that used The Essence of Onion, when he cooked. He hated onions too. I

feel like I have said this a million times. So ignore me. But if you like onion, add some onion.]
   iceberg lettuce [this is a substitute for celery]
   pickle [dill]
   pickled cheddar [see above]
   pickled jalapeño [see above]
   bacon [one slice]
   mayonnaise [two tbsp]
   mustard [Kind of one table-spoon. Don't do too much. To taste. I suppose.]
   salt and pepper
   nuts [if you remember]

Method:
Open can of tuna and let drain in sink.
Cut bacon into small slices and fry in frying pan on a medium heat.
Cut all ingredients into chunks.
Mix tuna with mayonnaise, salt and pepper, and mustard in bowl, with spoon.
Add chunked ingredients. Mix together.
When bacon is crispy spoon onto paper towel [save bacon grease in container for other things later on].
Add nuts to frying pan [if you remember this. I didn't, but I have frozen nuts in my freezer. Walnuts or pecans]. Toast.
Mix everything together.
Scoop onto bread to make a sandwich. Serve with a bowl of vegetable soup [see above, I think] and potato chips on the side.
Enjoy.

Stocks are up again. Invest in bacon and oil.

Morale has seemed to even out. Life goes on. People can't seem to even access the UnEmployment website to claim UnEmployment benefits. Which is not a good sign. The Hot Felon dumped some chicken bones out of a car window in the parking lot of a Ralph's. His relationship is still unknown with respect to Chloe Greene. He claims they are still on, but certain actions say otherwise. Like for instance, him, with an unknown female, eating chicken in a Ralph's parking lot.

Professor Curly doesn't find him very interesting unless Chloe is involved. I don't agree. Personally. I think he is an asshole. But he is being very smart about being the sociopath that he is. Not only that, but I think he had some work done on his hair. Which is funny because he always has a shaved head. And he is going bald. Or is bald. I think if he plays his card right he might be able to transfer to a whole new head of hair. And I think he is def playing his cards right.

Anyway. Nothing matters. The Yeah Yeah Yeahs are a rip-off of Siouxsie and the Banshees. They should own up to that. I do like their video, Maps, though. It reminds me that live performance is a valid enterprise.

But, so what?

Nobody really pays attention to anyone anyway. Not in earnest. Hold on, "What's that, Honey?"

Oh, shit! I gotta go! Professor Curly needs my help folding a towel. That girl. Am I right? She is a real fire-cracker!

Hasta la pasta!

DAY TWENTY-THREE

One fine morning in the month of May an elegant young horsewoman might have been riding a handsome sorrel mare along the flowery avenues of the Bois de Boulogne.

Hats off! Masks on!

Due to unpopular demand, this will no longer become a mystery novel. It was gonna be a good one, though. **The Plague** meets **Misery** with a little bit of **I Shall Bear Witness** by Victor Klemperer. But if a sequel happens?

Roller coaster of a day. Becca came by. Gave us the low-down on the high-up. From six feet away, of course. Things are rough all over. No way around it. Just had a flashback to a painting I did a few years ago. A woman showering on one side. On the other side she is handing out flowers to another woman. On the top I wrote: April Showers, Brings May Flowers. I wonder what happened to that. Pure gold.

I wonder what it would be like to live in a submarine for a couple months? Me and Professor

Curly are like ships in the night at this point. But only kind of. Like conjoined twins. Maybe? I mean, I don't think humans were meant to live like this, but we seem to be getting along pretty good, but things can get pretty intense, pretty fast. But then it is over again.

Leftovers for lunch. Leftovers for dinner. Soup. Pizza. Oxtail. Rice Pilaf. We need more supplies. Becca uses the same grocery store that we do. They said that there is now a line out the door due to social distancing. Going to go tomorrow. Could suck. Guess we will find out tomorrow.

Stocks started really high today. Ended in the red. Which means, down. Under where they started. Boris Johnson is still on life support. Turns out the Orange Douche has stock in the malaria drug he has been promoting. The fucking President is selling snake oil to the fucking American public during the fucking press briefings during a fucking pandemic. Did I mention he has stock in the snake oil company that makes the drug?

Had a dream that I was standing on top of an elevator shaft. The biggest elevator I had ever seen. And it was under construction. In the dream I was too afraid to look down the shaft. I also dreamed that I moved upstate into a room with two other dudes. The room was just three beds. Without sheets or pillows or blankets. I am really not looking forward to the financial fallout from this thing. The way the government is handling it makes me so so very nervous. The top doesn't need to be bailed out this time! It is the bottom. Meaning, us. Meaning the workers. It is like 2009 all over again, except they are stronger and we are weaker. Without a progressive agenda, we are screwed.

But it is nice to be able to have these thoughts in the middle of a pandemic. Rope-a-dope. Everything is rope-a-dope. It is exhausting. I don't have the energy to explain how bad things are going to get. The time that we had to deal with this crisis has come and gone. And because we live in a capitalistic state, everything, every single thing that is happening was preventable. Two of the most noticeable things:

1. Panicked private health care. Which means that premiums will skyrocket once this is over because the cost will be transferred to you, the consumer. And if you don't have insurance (which is something like 40 million people in America) and you get sick from this, well, bend over and kiss your future goodbye.

2. Rent. Rent will be deferred. Not absolved. Meaning, you can't work right now, so you can't pay rent, but instead of just putting rent on hold until this is finished, what will happen is your landlord will just tack on rent owed to future rent, so your rent will actually go up. And guess what happens when that happens in places like NYC

or LA or Chicago? All the people who don't need to live there and don't want to pay $2,000 dollars a month for some shitty studio apartment break lease and leave town. Which means the property value of everything drops. Which leads to both inflation and a second mass exodus. Leaving the cities in crisis. In depression. But you can also count on all the people that left the city looking for work in small towns and lesser populated areas. But these people tend to have more education and qualifications. So what happens there? Wages drop. Things like health insurance go away, because suddenly it is too expensive.

So now we got millions more people without a job, a place to live, and no health insurance. Combined with runaway inflation in inner cities. Then this just bounces back and forth, back and forth, until nothing. We are in another worldwide depression. And all it took was:

No living wage

No housing security

No health care for everyone

Which could have been avoided. They keep telling us that we are living our best lives. That humans haven't had it this good, ever. Not in the history of man. I think that is partially true. Clean sheets, clean towels. I can do a bunch of shit I never really wanted to do in the first place. Like, look at a screen all day that tells me people are pieces of shit. Or cunts, as Jack would say it. I would say it too, not to disparage Jack. Most people are cunts. But that is it. There is no upward trajectory. Or downward. Or sideward. If I am just going to be shit on all the time, then let it happen!

Give me these three things! Then let me be.

Living wage

Housing security

Health care

But for some reason we have to fight for it. Jeff Bezos just gave his wife, ex-wife, $36 billion dollars in their divorce agreement. And he is still the richest person in the world! In what bonkers world can you give somebody $36 billion dollars and still be the richest person? I am starting to think that Bill Gates is an idiot. And he is. I always had my suspicions, but. I mean he did do that thing a few years ago where he promised $100,000 dollars for the best new condom idea. Which, coming from a billionaire. I will let you lick my asshole if you design a better condom. And now he is spending billions of dollars of his own money to make a Coronavirus vaccine? Dudes! We need no more capitalism! Not now! Not ever! And if you think your ego can save us? You are an idiot!

At least Bezos has the temerity to be evil. And he will sell it back to us at $1,000 dollars a month in Amazon Bucks. Delivered monthly to our bank accounts. And we will lap it up.

Bezos 2020

DAY TWENTY-FOUR

Another roller coaster. Bernie dropped out. Unrelated, stocks way up. Just kidding. Not that stocks are up, the Unrelated part. Tacos Guggenheim for dinner. Fried corn tortillas. Ground beef. Tomato, jalapeño, onion and lemon juice salsa. Grated cheddar cheese. Iceberg lettuce. Homemade black beans on the side. Dessert of a couple chunks of frozen Snickers bar. Champagne. [Well, later]

What stinks about Bernie dropping out, aside from him dropping out, is that I never got a chance to vote. Or campaign. We were going to house somebody from his staff. But alas. A pandemic and a cruel world.

But then Professor Curly just got a Guggenheim!

It is a very topsy-turvy world we are living in. Went to make sure my library books didn't need to be renewed today. Online, of course. They are all good until June 1st. Which warmed my heart. I didn't have to renew them myself. It was automatic. Someone's looking out for me. Us.

Spent a couple hours today trying to get UnEmployment. The site only crashed six times. Not sure if it worked. Will find out tomorrow.

The grocery store was easy. No lines out the door. Maybe it was a different grocery store Becca was talking about. The jalapeños were in poor shape. Not much bacon. Or cold cuts. Tons of beer though. No flour tortillas. Decimated frozen section. People seemed less panicked. Resigned even. Resigned to what though, I don't know. Maybe they are resigned to the fact that the New York Times will run the headline:

Trump's Easter Miracle!

On Sunday. With no context. Even though 10,000 Americans will die between now and then. For no reason. South Korea has just north of 200 deaths from this thing. They have 1/5th the population that we do. Adjusted for that, it would be just north of 1,000 deaths. American deaths: 15,000. First confirmed cases on the same day. And mind you, the Republicans are blaming democracy for this. Because America has too much democracy in its bones. But if you look at the Democracy Index. The way that they rank liberty and freedom in countries around the world. America is #25. South Korea is #23. Just sayin.

Don't mean to be so negative. Not feeling very optimistic. I think the Biden campaign should start handing out little bottles of lube that say Biden 2020 on them. That way we can keep our buttholes moist. Or I don't know, maybe that is what Trudeau was talking about when he was talking about, "Moist words"?

Being an American sucks right now. But I am too old to be punk and just ignore everything, but I am too young to die. I don't want to move to Canada, but Mexico would be all right. But both those countries hate Americans. And for good reason. And as much as I love Brooklyn, things are going to get bad. Very bad. Late 70's bad. And if Biden's running mate isn't young, and black, and female. I mean. The goal posts just fell over. Ideology just went out the window. It is a race to the bottom. And since the person whose response to whether or not he would cut Social Security is:

C'mon, Bernie!

I don't have much hope that he can take the

constant barrage of shit-slinging that is about to explode onto his ass. But who knows? Michelle Obama? Stacey Abrams? I will do whatever is possible to get the Democratic nominee elected. And this will be the last time I talk pure shit about Joe Biden, but:

C'mon, Joe!

A gaffe machine to the max. Who has nothing but bad moves in his past. Corporate Democrat. Will get torn to shreds by the RNC. And as much as the Corporate Media is so very willing to go against Bernie for their own purposes, they will gleefully destroy Biden the same way that they did Hillary. There is no doubt in my mind. But if they can put someone there behind Biden, someone to look at when shit goes side-wise, like a picture of a loved one that you can look at when you are gang-raped.

We need it. We all need it. There is no end to this mayhem. But all they have to do is sow discord. To make it seem like none of this matters. Because you are fucked either way. And they are right. And they will win because of it. And wouldn't you rather support a winner?

I don't know. I hope the DNC knows what they are doing. And I will now support whatever happens. Although my street cred just plummeted because Professor Curly got a Guggenheim in the middle of a pandemic! And we are just lucky enough to have all of our hard work to peak at just the right time.

I will put everything I can to use for this election. This maniac that is in charge now is the greatest threat to what we consider a democracy since the very beginning. He will destroy it if he gets re-elected. Millions of people will die. If not more.

Biden 2020

DAY TWENTY-FIVE

No roller coaster. Made another loaf. Starting to get the hang of it. Three loaves now. My slippery fingers getting down into the greasy tender folds. Thrusting my thick, gigantic rolling-pin upon the very kneady flesh. Squirting fantastic flavors into Professor Curly's gaping mouth.

I do wonder what this quarantine is doing to my figure. I can't remember the last time I ate this much bread. I haven't gone on a walk in two days. There is a pair of binoculars by the front window. There is nothing to look at though. Joggers, I guess. Fast and boring. Maybe an occasional hard nip, or a swinging sweatpants dangler.

Stocks, up. UnEmployment, doubled. Deaths, rising. None of it connects. Maybe none of it ever connected. Like, maybe, it was never connected. And all that is happening now is just a debunking of the system we have decided was reality? But that is just junk science. Like a Malcolm Gladwell article.

K2 interview tomorrow at 830a MST

[Mountain Standard Time] or 1030a EST [Eastern Standard Time]. Me and Billy Floyd. C'mon, Floyd. Tune in. Just joking. I have no idea how you could do that. I will send pictures.

Send nudes.

Washed my hair. And conditioned. Growing a pimple on my nose. Tried to watch a documentary on the Great Depression last night. Very depressing. Turns out an investment in infrastructure, a living wage, and job security would prevent almost all the financial problems that happen in a capitalist society. But I guess we will never learn. Or will we? This sort of thinking is why I believe Jeff Bezos will emerge from this crisis as the king of the world. He is definitely evil. He is definitely greedy. But I don't think he is stupid.

He already did the living wage. Although, I would argue that that is not true. But it is closer than $7.50/hr. He is already working towards a better infrastructure. He just needs to get involved with maintenance. Which will be easy when the Government goes bankrupt here shortly. The only thing left is job security. Which will be hard for his fragile ego to wrap his mind around, but he will come to terms with it. Because he will understand that as much as he hates the idea of sick leave and vacation time and personal days, he will understand that One Trillion Dollars is equal to One Thousand Billion Dollars. And if he just keeps his dick in his pants for long enough he will get what he wants. Which is ALL the money.

What the hell happened to that guy? I mean, I question my personal value when I make $40/hr, like whether I deserve it or not. I mean, his insecurity. My god. If someone hugged him on purpose and with love, he would probably, literally, explode. Or stab them to death for exposing his weakness. Or more likely, just hire somebody to ruin their life so he can convince himself that all humans are trash and deserve to die.

But I digress.

I am now officially excited for the future. It is hyperbolic that Jeff Bezos can save us from this mess. And we crossed the Rubicon when the Orange Douche got elected. But now that the world as we know it is gone. That for some reason the powers that be think we can just get back to normal when this is over. That the Rubicon, once a metaphor, is now an actual river that just became a horrible monster that has peeled itself from the earth, and has grown arms made of fire, and destruction, and is about to start destroying everything we hold dear. I don't know. I feel up for the task.

I feel sober. Relaxed. Default on your loans. Don't pay your taxes. Don't pay your rent. Don't go back to work. Fuck them all. We don't live in a meritocracy. All those fuckers who think they earned their money through hard work and what not, they didn't. They have no idea what to do right now. For good reason. They never had any idea what to do in the first place!

They were lucky.

Money makes lice.

Vote blue. It is the only way out of this. But the panic and confusion that is coming in the next few weeks is going to create such an insane response from the right that I don't even know how it will transpire. All of the adults have left the room. Which will cause the status quo to panic too. And because they all need the working class to be working or nothing will work, they will be screaming at us to pull ourselves up by our bootstraps double-time. But we can't! We can't work when there is no work!

Part of me thinks we should spend any extra money we have from the stimulus package that comes to us on progressive candidates. Like, for instance, Amy McGrath, who is Moscow Mitch's challenger in Kentucky. That would be the ultimate, Fuck You! to this lawless and corrupt administration. She has a good chance to win. Moscow Mitch is very unpopular in Kentucky. And he is a piece of shit. And, arguably more powerful than the Orange Douche.

If we even get that money.

Why do Republicans hate the American people? Don't they have neighbors?

DAY TWENTY-SIX

Funny day. Started with a video interview with K2 and ended with making hot dog buns. Both turned out great. Talked to my mom. She told me the craziest story[1] about these two Mikes from Worland. Cousins.

So like a week ago my mom was going to bed. She checked the temperature. It was 9 degrees F. But they said it felt like -4 degrees F. Which is pretty cold. That same night in another part of town, this one Mike had gone to bed early. Like 8p. He and his wife. Well around 930p this Mike gets a phone call. From a number he doesn't recognize. He was asleep when the phone rang, so he answered it thinking it might be an emergency. The guy on the other end said:

"Are you Mike [X]?"

"Yes, who is this?"

"Who lives at [X]?"

---

[1]. Disclaimer: This is my version of a story my mom told me over the phone. All quotes are my own. Nothing is verbatim.

"Yes, who is this?"

"This is [X]. I got your number from [X]. I will be there in three hours."

"No you won't. I think you got the wrong number, buddy."

"No sir. You are Mike [X] who lives at [X] I got your number from [X]."

"I don't know you. Or him. Don't come over."

"But my information is correct."

"Yeah, well. Maybe you are looking for my cousin. We have the same name."

"Well, can you give me his address?"

"I don't have it."

"Why not?"

"Because he doesn't like me very much. Don't come over."

So Mike goes back to sleep. Three hours later there is a knock on the door. Mike and his wife get up and peak out of the curtains. A car with its headlights on in the driveway. Neither he or his wife answer the door. The car drives away. Two hours after that the doorbell rings frantically. This time they get up and call the police. They let the guy in. Speculation, because this is Wyoming, Mike is holding a gun. The guy is obviously freezing. He has a duffel bag and a backpack. The cops show up. The guy tells them this convoluted story about taking a plane from Newark to D.C. then another one to Florida and then to Chicago, then Denver, then finally to Casper. Where he called Mike and then took a cab ride for three hours to get to Worland. The cops ask the couple if they want to press charges. They say they don't. He didn't actually do anything. Can't they just put him in jail for the night and deal with this tomorrow? The cops say they can't unless they press charges. So the couple presses charges and the cops take the guy to jail for the night. With both his bags.

In the morning the wife goes outside and notices that Mike's construction trailer is open. Inside is another duffel bag and some fried chicken.

Later that day one of the cops calls Mike. He asks whether or not he still wants to press charges. Mike says no, and that there is another duffel bag the guy left behind. And some fried chicken. The cop laughs and mentions that the guy tried to get them to go back and get the chicken the night before because he was really hungry. He then tells Mike that the guy tested positive for Coronavirus. And he and his wife should probably quarantine for fourteen days.

And that is how Coronavirus made it to Worland, Wyoming.

There are other details I am sure I missed. And some details I never got. Like, why was the guy going to Wyoming specifically? Like, what was he doing in New York? Was he young? Old? How much does a cab ride from Casper to Worland cost? Are the cops now on quarantine? What about the cab driver? What happened to the fried chicken? Did Mike ever talk to his cousin, Mike?

Fried Cabbage For Hot Dogs:
Take half a frozen cabbage from your freezer. Thaw on top of radiator. Slice into thick slices. Put into pot. Add three big pinches of coarse Kosher salt. Quite a few grinds of fresh black pepper. A bunch of anise seeds. A quarter cup of white vinegar. Cook on medium high until liquid is gone. Stir often. Remove from heat. Let sit.

Zesty!

No stocks today. Good Friday. Good Friday wisdom:

Any burrito can be a breakfast burrito if you eat it in the morning.

The interview went good. Billy Floyd is hilarious. He is also really good at his job. I think he has a future.

Hot dog buns are a weird endeavor. They were a success, but they need more work. I didn't have a pastry brush for the egg wash, so I had to fashion one out of a paper towel cut into strips and a bread tie. Worked perfect. MacGyver would have been proud. Or Alton Brown. Although Alton Brown is more of a, repurpose this other tool for cooking use, kind of guy. Not a, use what you have to solve a complex problem, kind of guy. But that reminds me of this dream I had:

I was an assistant to this "Master" chef and he

had a "Secret" store that he went to to get his "Unique" ingredients. I was driving his car for him. When we got there, he ordered "Two flat-footed ducks." Well, it turned out that the "Unique" store needed a dishwasher. And because all the "Chefs" shopped there I could also write articles about "High-end" cooking. I just had to do all the dishes first. And there were a lot of dishes to do!

DAY TWENTY-SEVEN

French toast and bacon for brunch. Saturday. Did some bed bonin' in the afternoon. Forgot to mention some bonin' that happened the other day. It was a little one sided, so I am not sure if it counts as bonin' or not. But it did happen. Leftovers for dinner. Pasta and peas with bacon and fried nuts. Pecans. Also, found a use for broccoli stems. Chicken Back Po Boys for lunch.

Broccoli Shavings With A Chicken Garlic Stock Reduction:
1/4 cup chicken stock
1 garlic clove
2 broccoli stems
tbsp olive oil
large frying pan
red pepper flakes
salt and pepper
peeler
knife
tongs

Chop ends off of broccoli stems. Peel outer skin. Add to the stock you are cooking. If you are cooking a stock. If you are not cooking a stock, do something else with them.

Take remaining stems and whittle down to nothing with the peeler. Broccoli stems are almost useless to cook with. They are stringy. And meaty. And tend to be flavor-less.

Turn heat to medium under frying pan. Add oil. Add broccoli shavings. Salt and pepper. Red pepper flakes. Fry. Stir often with tongs.

Peel and slice garlic clove. Then chop.

Cook shavings until slightly browned. Add stock and garlic. Reduce until liquid is gone.

Serve in a bowl with a fork.

Yum.

I would write down the Chicken Back Po Boy recipe, but I learned today that chicken backs are useless for sandwich meat. Which is ironic. To me. Can something be ironic only to oneself? I feel like there must be a better word for that. I mean. Chicken kind of grosses me out. But if I am going to eat chicken, I like to eat chicken wings. But chicken wings are mostly skin and fat. Very little meat. But making a sandwich out of chicken skin and chicken fat doesn't really work. And chicken backs are just the same as chicken wings. Skin, fat, and very little meat. Therefore, if you are going to make a chicken sandwich you should use the breast or the thigh. Chicken. Otherwise you should just dip your fried chicken backs in mayonnaise and eat it off the bone. Which seems a little much. Even by my standards. But hey, these are special times.

Talked to my brother Luke today. Up there in Portland, Maine. Via computer phone. His two kids have wonderful haircuts. He tells me there will be a shortage of CO2 soon. Which should have some devastating effects on certain commerce [which I need to look into]. Also, the Pope blames the queers for climate change. Becca, I am looking in your direction. Just joking. Both with Becca and the Pope. I don't know what the Pope said. I should look it up. I just hate the Catholic church so much. The only thing they could do to make me want to give the Pope two seconds of my time would be if the Pope stood next to the Orange Douche on live TV and blew his brains out. After the Orange Douche did it first. Of course.

But then I just spent three minutes writing about how I refuse to give the Pope any of my time. Shit! Now I am doing it again!

Haircut tomorrow! Although, it occurs to me that my daughter can finally stay over, starting Tuesday. Maybe I should wait. So she can film it. I will do a reading. Professor Curly can cut it. Maybe she can use the golden scissors the Guggenheim Foundation sent her with the giant check she received, and the personal letter from David Byrne and Patti Smith saying, Congrats! You finally made it! Welcome to the club! Frigus manus a mortuis!

To go back to the Pope, though. A progressive

Pope is better than a regressive Pope. And I understand that there are billions of Catholics in the world. I still don't care. Practically or pragmatically. It all sounds like, to me, David Duke coming out and saying, I am in favor of integration in schools, now. That dog don't hunt. Ask me again in twenty years. Five years. Next year. Shit, next week even. The damage you have done can't be undone. Not in this century. And probably the next. But it is not like they burn my books in my own home town, right? Oh, right, they do. Let's all eat a ham for Jesus.

The days are getting longer. I yelled, Boobs! today out of our back window. Professor Curly was sitting on the bed, reading a book. The neighbors a few houses over looked up. That was pretty funny. I hid by the radiator.

Professor Curly drank two tiny thimbles of champagne at dinner, and got drunk. That was very cute. Lightweight/early bird. I think she might only drink champagne now. I have no idea where she gets the bottles from. Although, she did go to the Post Office today. Supposedly to return a pair of lousy looking yoga pants. Maybe the Guggenheim Foundation mailed her a fresh bottle? I don't think we will ever know.

Twenty-three rolls of toilet paper left. There is now a box of tissues on top of the toilet. Next to the candle. I don't see this ending well.

But I am surprised. We have been able to keep

our humours to ourselves. Mostly. A couple hiccups here and there. But nothing dramatic. Maybe the Catholic church and American democracy CAN work together. Church and State. Too bad I have to spend an hour each morning using a rock I found by the tree out front scrubbing skid-marks out of her panties before she lets me make her breakfast.

Just joking! I promised I wouldn't break the wall!

If I was less mature I would say something like, Oh, Yeah! like the Kool-Aid Man as he breaks through the brick wall. But I am an adult. So:

Honey! Can you hand me the rock hammer? We got a stubborn chunker!

Oh, Yeah!

DAY TWENTY-EIGHT

Four weeks. Easter. Beef roast. Roast potatoes with onions. Asparagus. Garlic toast. Cadbury egg for dessert. The last of the champagne.

> Garlic Powder:
> 4 cloves of garlic
> small frying pan
> knife
> glass cup with flat bottom
> cutting board

Place frying pan on stovetop and set to low heat. Like the 2 setting if electric. As little flame as possible if gas.

Cut wart ends off of garlic cloves. Peel. Don't smash. Slice into thin slices. As thin as you can get, but no need to get crazy. Place into frying pan. Cook. It is possible that they will stick. Just push around with a spoon or whatever.

The idea is to dry the garlic out without cooking it too much.

Eventually the garlic slices will start to act like

dried banana chips. Remove from frying pan and chop. Put back into frying pan. Cook.

Repeat this process. It is slow going. I have no idea how long it takes. Frankly, I was just killing time when I did this. I was making a meat rub, and I needed some powdered garlic. But it does seem important not to rush. Otherwise you will burn the garlic. Nothing is more bitter than a burnt garlic clove. If you believe that, you haven't met my ex-wife. Oh, yeah!

Eventually the garlic becomes dried out. At this point you can start to rub it under the glass cup with a flat bottom. The garlic that is ready to powder will powder. The garlic that still needs to cook will remain gummy. Just scrape the gum up and continue to cook in the frying pan.

If you have ever made lines of cocaine, now is the time to put that knowledge to use. If you haven't ever made lines of cocaine, use your imagination. The idea is to get the granules of garlic as small as possible. Rub with the bottom of the glass cup. Scrape together with your knife. Repeat.

Eventually you will have a nice mound of powdered garlic. I put half of the mound that I made into a bowl with equal parts kosher salt and black pepper. Which was enough rub to cover a 3 lb hunk of beef for roasting. I put the remaining garlic powder in a small container with a lid. For later use.

Jesus would be 2,053. If he were alive today. Think of that! That's pretty old. And now Bob Dylan finally has a number one hit. After all his years of obscurity. He is like 78. You work hard enough. Long enough. The American Dream!

I think I need to go back to my old diet. Beans and tortillas. All this weird food is making me anxious. It is like, somewhere between my mouth and my butthole some old couple from Yonkers drove down to the city to see some Broadway show and are trying to parallel park in Midtown:

Go forward! What? I said, go forward! [rolls down window] What? I said, go forward! Stop! Back up! What? I said, back up! What? Turn! No, the other way! The husband is driving. The wife is standing on the sidewalk. Making hand gestures. The husband has his head out the driver side window. I think it started raining! What?

That is life for you. You either shit your pants, or you throw up. There is no in-between.

DAY TWENTY-NINE

Professor Curly has rickets. She gets plenty of D. Just not enough Vitamin D. She has been trying out this new method she calls, The Bendy Wrist. Heavy rain all day. Stocks down. Philly cheese steaks for lunch. Chicken gyro for dinner. Made a pita bread that was kind of a tortilla/hot-dog bun/bread loaf hybrid. The recipe was good, but how I cooked it was wrong. Baked, not right. Crispy. Stove top flash-cook, closer, but not quite right. I think I may need to cook them in the oven at a very high heat for a short amount of time. Or a wood stove. Watered the plants.

The interview came out great! I am telling you, Billy Floyd has chops. Brian too!

Wyoming Author Quarantined In New York

Feel a little bit bad for my mom. People in Wyoming watch the news. She has been getting texts all day. Saying stuff like, Saw your son on the TV! I didn't know he was a writer. I want to read his books now! Which would be just fine if she lived in say, Dayton, Ohio, but she works for the BLM [Bureau of Land Management], and! my home town is 5,000 people. Some of my books are a little racy. And she is mentioned in a few of them. She has to live there. But, and like I have said many times to her: I never asked to be born, Mom!

UnEmployment benefits came in. $323 + $600 = $923 dollars. I guess per week. Kind of hard to process. I have been Stockholm Syndromed for so long by the American System that I only feel guilt. But I literally can't work. And I feel like I am committing fraud. The cops will show up any day now. And the only three markets open right now are, Rent, Groceries, and Illicit Drugs. But deep down in my heart I know that Amazon paid $0 dollars in income tax last year. So philosophically, I am okay with a personal bailout. But my asshole isn't sore and my face isn't covered in jizz, so, who knows?

The new running theory is that Amazon will take over the USPS [United States Postal Service]. Because the Orange Douche refuses to fund them. Which is an irony on irony crime. Meaning. If the President won't fund the USPS because Amazon is personally benefiting from its government assistance, and by de-funding the USPS means it either goes bankrupt, or a private corporation takes over the financial responsibilities, and if that private corporation is Amazon. I mean. I just got a little under a thousand dollars from the government and because I am so poor I feel like that is a large amount of money, which means I am stupid, because I am poor, and even I can see that the USPS has been around since 1775. And having control of that business, especially when we know that package delivery will be how we are going to do commerce for at least the next twenty years, fifty years? I don't know. Either everyone in charge is a complete moron, or everyone in charge is a blithering idiot. You just handed border security to El Chapo. I can't think of a person who would have a greater vested interest in getting the USPS to run more smoothly than Jeff Bezos. And combine that with two hundred and fifty years of development? You just handed him a giant slab of marble, a chisel, a hammer, and said, Okay, Michelangelo, do us a self portrait!

But the other candidate is Walmart. But Bezos will own Walmart by Christmas. Why go to them when they can come to you?

But what the hell do I know? I just had to tell the UnEmployment Office I have "some college" because I went to the University of Wyoming for a semester. I don't think the Pulitzer Foundation will take my application if I write in that I have "some college." Do you think you can win an award for, "Outsider Journalism"? Although I would argue that it would be, "Non-Typical Journalism," but who is going to be on board with that? David Sedaris would. But only if he won the award first. That kid is a slut.

Tomorrow my daughter is coming over for a couple days. She is bringing Shiver, her cat, six artichokes, and a hand-held phone attachment so Professor Curly can get on the horn without it hurting her ears. Excited!

I think she will just plop on the couch and play her video game. Eating apple slices and making sassy remarks. Can't wait. Although the logistics of this apartment leave something to be desired. A zesty redhead and a cool dude conjoined twins, ships in the night, is one thing. Add a cat and a sassy twelve-year-old. It is going to be capacity!

I should probably get some macaroni and cheese.

DAY THIRTY

G moved in. My daughter. Brought her cat, Shiver. Three artichokes. One gallon of black beans. Tacos for lunch. Pizza for dinner. Stocks are up. G took the ante-room. I get the kitchen. Professor Curly gets the bedroom.

  New Schedule:
    7a PC wakes
    7a-10a PC time
    10a Joey and G free to leave private quarters
    130p Lunch
    2p-630p Free time
    630p Dinner
    7p PC and G to private quarters
    7p-10p Joey time
    10p Lights out
    10p-7a Sleep

I know it probably seems like I run a tight ship, but now is not the time for a lack of discipline. Three people and a cat in a 1 1/2 bedroom apartment in the middle of a pandemic quarantine. In the middle of the pandemic epicenter. I guess we will see how tomorrow goes. May need to make adjustments.

Fender bender out front. They called the cops. Which I find very irritating. A young couple, kind of bumped into the back of this older [older meaning, not middle aged, but older than the other couple] couple. There was no damage that I could see. But money. And cars. And America. The older couple was a big guy with a beard and a shaved head. Making sure that the other couple didn't drive away. His partner was on the phone with the cops. Standing up behind their car. She said, Yeah, you should send an ambulance. My back and my neck kind of hurt. The young couple was pleading with them to just let it go. There wasn't any damage. Then the guy with the shaved head said, Whatever man, you were disrespectful when you got out of the car. I don't care. We gotta call the cops.

Ten minutes later. The cops show up. Gloves on. Masks on. Oh, I forgot to mention this interaction between the two couples happened in the middle of the street. The aggrieved couple leaving their car in the middle of the street. For the cops to see. Nobody wearing a mask. Or gloves. So when the cops show up they tell the aggrieved couple to pull the car to the side. So traffic can go by.

At that point I got so annoyed I stopped watching. The cops. I mean, I can't stand cops. They are the worst. But at the moment, they are putting their lives on the line in order to maintain order in the middle of a crisis. And this is the shit that they have to deal with? I mean, the cops are getting sick because some asshole feels disrespected by some other asshole? It really is not cool. Cops are dying because of these kinds of interactions.

Car insurance. Capitalism.

I think it might be time to re-examine the purpose of the police force. Fender benders? I think that insurance companies should have their own police force that they send out on these calls. But how would that work? Maybe the insurance companies should give money to the municipalities? But won't premiums go up? I guess they would. But should tax money be going into paying for things like cops micro-managing grievances? Just so the insurance companies have something on record? So they can't be sued? I don't know. I really don't know.

What I do know is that cops should stop arresting people of color for non-violent drug offences. That cops shouldn't be handing out tickets for people jumping the turnstiles. Abolish turnstiles. That there Should Not be for-profit prisons. Anywhere. Ever. That going to prison should be the very last option for any offender. Americans should not live in fear of the State. It does not decrease crime. It does the opposite. Crime increases when you believe you live in an unjust society. And for good reason. That reason is:

Fuck You!

But Joey, you ask, you run a tight ship. Isn't that a micromanaging of grievances? You don't know the riff-raff I surround myself with. They look cute when you see them, but you turn your back for one second. Bam! Logs all day! I'm bored. Let's do something. I'm hungry. Why don't we have any more toilet paper? Where is the clean underwear? Suddenly I am not so much the insane one. Am I?

I run a tight ship for your own good. That's why.

You'll thank me later.

DAY THIRTY-ONE

Things are ship-shape. One addition: 330p-430p Radio Hour and, "Sleep" has been replaced with, "Sack Time." Tacos for lunch. Hot dogs for dinner. Fresh made hot dog buns. Worked a little better the second time. Cherry Diet Coke for Professor Curly at lunch. Just added frozen cherries. In addition to ice. Rice pilaf with the Easter asparagus. Cutting board is starting to warp. I think I will have to iron it tomorrow. Too much use. Frozen blueberry waffles and bacon for breakfast. With orange juice.

Stocks are down. Stimulus checks are delayed because the Orange Douche needs his names on the checks. Bezos has made $24 billion dollars since January. He will be worth $200 billion dollars personally by the end of June. $300 billion dollars by the end of the summer.

G is a hoot. Shiver is a hoot. Professor Curly is a stick in the mud. Just jokes. She is a hoot too. New development out the back window. Cute MILF with a 4-year-old and playground in the backyard.

Paunchy middle aged husband businessman. They share a fence with a twenties tattooed hunk with a dog. When it is sunny outside he does yard work shirtless. Professor Curly said she saw him pumping iron with a two-by-four. My theory is that things end in scandal when she gets caught one night jumping the fence to do some bonin'. But our window will probably be open. So we will hear it all. Maybe even see it.

Out of potatoes. Burned the last batch. Well, more like dried them out. I knew I was baking them too long. I just didn't do anything about it. That is my problem with potatoes. They are difficult to cook. And they taste gross. The way I usually tell when a potato is done is when it sticks to the bottom of the trash can. I should have checked them when I thought about it. I didn't. I am sorry. I put them in some water to soak. Maybe I can reconstitute them and serve them for breakfast. It wouldn't surprise me if the best potato was the potato that you burned and then soaked in water and then let sit overnight and then fried with onions and eggs in the morning. Stupid potatoes.

We also had an artichoke for dinner. Success. I suppose. G and Professor Curly gobbled the whole thing down. Simmered the thing for like 50 minutes. I thought the last time I had an artichoke was back in '96 but Professor Curly and G reminded me that we had one in Harlem like a year and a half ago. I usually can tell an artichoke is done when the hole in your grocery bag is big enough for it to fall onto the sidewalk.

We officially have to wear masks in public. Under penalty of citation. When in a circumstance where we can't maintain six feet of distance. Meaning, everyone is now wearing masks. Strangely comforting to see people finally taking this seriously. First feeling of hope since this lockdown started.

Professor Curly's mom got UnEmployment. Which is great. She was freaking out. For good reason. She is 78. Works in Real Estate. Has almost no savings. Lives in New Hampshire. Translation: You are on your fucking own. Live free or die. Not, live freely or die. More, If you can't afford to live, die. The Boot-Strap State. Even if you are 78 and have worked your entire life.

G made whisked coffee today. I just happened to have instant coffee because of the work I do with Scott. Living in hotel rooms. Et cetera. Don't know if it was tasty or not. The smell of the instant coffee made me anxious. Like I needed to set my alarm for 5a after forcing myself to go to bed at 12a. It also made me nostalgic for writing, ***Elmira***. That book had potential. Maybe I can convince Professor Curly to buy a house in that town with all her Art Monies.

She just got nominated for some award. Her play. Her directing. The main actress [actor].

Sound design. Not sure what award it was. Not sure if it is important or not. But like a jerk I said, Oh! the award ceremony will be online, I said:

"The only thing I can think of that would be worse than going to a theater award ceremony would be to go to an award ceremony online."

"But Joey, you don't understand, me and Emily live for free champagne and hors d'oeuvres!"

Then I felt like the jerk I am.

Because she actually enjoys things.

But then I get annoyed. Not that there is an online awards ceremony or even awards at all, but still, in the middle of the world crashing to the ground there are things like the New York Times publishing hot lists of podcasts to listen to. In the middle of a fucking pandemic they are still the fucking gate keepers. This last issue of The New Yorker added **On The Boards TV** to things to watch. Which is great. Because they have been recording their performances for years and years. And some of the best theater in the whole world goes through there. In Seattle. But it takes a global meltdown for them to mention that? They should have promoted this years ago. Ran a feature. But who knows? Maybe they did. I don't remember seeing it. And my other point is that I, me personally, I can't even get a Wikipedia page because I haven't been written about in these publications. I don't have the citations. Which is annoying as shit. I could give two shits about them writing about me, but I would like to have a Wikipedia page. It would help me sell books. Frustrating.

To this day if I mention that you can buy my books on Amazon people say, Oh, really? Like that is an impressive thing. But they don't actually want to talk about it. How on one side it is great that you can get a book published and sell it on Amazon and they will print it for you for cheap, but on the other side that means you are killing local and small publishing houses. But then they always follow that question with, Self published? Which makes you feel double gross. And tired.

But that is the point of the Wikipedia page. It doesn't really matter. It is just a beefed up Google search. A localized Google search. And it is helpful. It is. But so what. Like everything else, by the time it matters it will be too late for you to give a shit about it.

You're either ten years too late, or ten years too early. Story of my life. Against all odds.

But then G said something pretty funny earlier. I was trying to get her to eat some of the asparagus rice at lunch. She said she doesn't care for asparagus. I said she should just try it. And she said:

"Eating asparagus turns your body into that horrible bathroom spray you have, but in reverse. You eat it and bad smells come out."

Pretty funny.

DAY THIRTY-TWO

Thursday. Stocks neither up nor down. Tacos for lunch. Pancakes with blueberries for breakfast. Leftover pizza and macaroni and cheese with hot dogs for dinner. G's mom stopped by to bring some clean underpants. On her bike. She also brought a phone handle for Professor Curly. Pink with sparkles. Belongs to G. I got it for her like four years ago. From a fashion shoot. Professor Curly's ears were hurting. Because of her ear buds. And all the talking on the phone she does.

The Pew foundation just pushed Professor Curly's award back until next July. Guess we won't be moving to Philly any time soon. The house in Vermont that we were thinking about maybe looking at just got taken off the market. Turns out it was river adjacent. Too bad. Housing futures look really bonkers at the moment.

I'd imagine there will be a mass exodus out of the city. 25%? I mean, rent is impossible here if you can't work. And breaking a rental lease is not really that big of a deal. There is no national database. I don't think there is even a citywide database that would mean that you would suffer any consequence. Just the loss of a deposit. Which is nothing when you are looking at losing that much money every single month for the foreseeable future. And then the people that do the renting? The renters? If they are smart, which I doubt they are, they will just absolve rents until the lockdown is over. But because by the nature of the business, I am sure they will be greedy, which means that they will just defer payment. And add a percentage of lost rents to the future rent payments. So:

Rent prices will go up for people who choose to stay here. And at the same time the market will suddenly have 25% more apartments for rent. Which will drop market value. Which will cause some pretty big confusion. Hurt feelings. Resentment. And terrible behavior.

And if you think that will just mean that rich people will just move in gobble up buildings and totally take over, well, I think you are wrong. Nobody is going to move into the city in the middle of a pandemic just to get a hot deal. I am sure there will be some people. But those people will be dumb.

And what about all those people that left the city? Moving back in with mom and dad? People who were saving money to buy an apartment in the city where the value is super inflated?

Suddenly they can buy a house in rural Vermont that has been on the market for two years. And have $200,000 dollars to live off for the next however many years?

See what I am getting at here?

Professor Curly and I are really lucky. We don't need to pay rent for three months. And we haven't signed a new lease. I am thinking we just wait it out and then renegotiate. And now that we won't move to Philly for over a year. Also, we haven't heard from the landlord in almost two months. Maybe we just squat the place.

We got a new mailman. Hopefully it is just because the other one has some time off. But the new one doesn't seem like he has done the route before. I have never seen him before. And doesn't seem used to the houses. I can't imagine how stressful that job must be right now.

Also, mail related, we got an envelope from UPS [United Parcel Service] which is not the USPS [United States Postal Service]. The address is correct, but the name is wrong. I left it with the neighbors yesterday. They gave it right back. Professor Curly just kicked it down the front steps for some reason. I brought it inside. It is from some health care provider out in California. Chico. I called the number on the package. Left a message with somebody named Paula. She called me back. Told me to just send it back. But that's the thing. Do I just drop it in the USPS mail box?

Return to sender? Or do I try and find a UPS store to send it back? I can't say that I care enough to do that. I would love to help these guys out, but I don't think I am willing to expose myself to this virus so some guy that gave this company the wrong address can fill out some paperwork. I asked Paula if she would call the guy, and get a correct address and call me back, and she said, We will just track the package. Whatever that means. I guess tomorrow I will just drop it in the USPS drop box, and hope for the best.

The cutting board is floating in the bathtub. I was wrong about being able to iron it. I will now soak it until 10p and then weigh it down for a few days. Luckily Charley made us a cutting board for Christmas. Which is excellent, and beautiful, but a little on the small side. Kind of like him. Just jokes. He is a big, beastly, bulging man.

It was a very uneventful day. Very wonderful to spend it with G, and Professor Curly, and, Shiver. Not sure if Shiver has eaten any mouses yet. But I hope so. I had some dream that she was eating her own turds. Whatever that means. Somebody had put all her turds in a bowl next to her food. I also keep having these dreams about elevators dropping to the ground. And sleeping giants. But also about this woman that liked to masturbate to an audience when this guy whispered predictions of doom in her ear. While the cleaning lady was taking a shower. And Ilan [Stony Lonesome] being afraid the government could read his finger prints in the dough when he was kneading bread. He is the only person I know in New York that owns a gun. I am sure there are others. He is the only one that talks about it.

The haircut, tomorrow. Today got bonked because G had a tutoring session during Free Time. But I even washed, and conditioned my hair.

Living near the beach chair.

DAY THIRTY-THREE

TGIF. Pancakes with blueberries for breakfast. Bacon. Artichoke, and cucumber sandwiches for lunch. Tacos Guggenheim for dinner. With red drink and PeriProsecco. Stocks up.

Cutting board is flat. I flattened the curve. It's like a metaphor for the quarantine.

Got half a haircut. The back half. Maybe get the rest tomorrow.

Had a dream that somebody dropped a black wolf off at my doorstep. In a box. Then ran away yelling, You are going to have to deal with this for a really long time! Then I ran inside and locked the door. Then a zombie showed up and screamed so loud the glass broke. Then I woke up.

I really wish that anyone, anyone! else was leading the response to this crisis. This is getting really exhausting. It feels like the Mueller Report was released, then Bill Barr did all his lying, and then Mueller testified before Congress all day, every day, and on loop. I know I shouldn't pay such close attention, but come on! Somebody has to be a witness to this shit. Now is not a time to be complacent. Not that there is ever a good time to be complacent, but right now is definitely not that time.

For instance, it was Betsy Fucking DeVos that funded the campaign to get the people in Michigan to do their idiotic protest! The current fucking Secretary Of Education! I feel like my head is a balloon and somebody glued googly eyes on it. That is what my brain feels like. Or that monkey flying a kite that I saw earlier. Which was pretty good. But even that monkey was able to pull the kite down to safety. And nobody knows how it got the kite in the air in the first place. I very much know how I got here.

I remember my brother Charley telling me he was surprised that I gave a shit back in the summer of 2017. He also told me most people in Wyoming just plugged their noses when they voted in 2016. I remember thinking that the idea of just plugging your nose to vote for somebody was insane. Oh how naive I was!

But then Wyoming voted overwhelmingly for the Orange Douche. I think they had the highest percentage in favor. But then he is exactly the nightmare he was predicted to be. And as much as most of the Wyoming population has its head up its ass, they really don't like to be bullied. Which is a good thing. However…

I am really starting to think that Mitt Romney will make a third party run.

199 days.

And when Biden announces Sarah Palin as his running mate on Sunday. I am writing in Howard Dean.

I am joking! Vote Biden. His campaign is sending out Biden 2020 nose plugs, ear plugs, and butt plugs. Stay safe! Comdoms. No glove, no love.

But really! Vote Biden! This is serious!

We don't have the luxury to experiment at the moment!

Meat prices are starting to go up. Because the Red states aren't taking this pandemic seriously and people are dying from working at processing plants. Causing them to shut down. Ground beef is now $2 dollars more per pound than they were just two days ago. This is tragic. Very tragic. And pointless. Nobody needs to die so I can eat a ground beef taco. But this will force us to eat more of a plant based diet. Which is good for the environment. But a piece of meat is so much better for protein than a bunch of beans. People are already starving. This woman today. When I was at the grocery store. Mask on. Gloves. Just staring at the ground beef. Shaking her head, Are you serious? She looked at me. I said, It's gonna get worse. I imagine she frowned, but who knows. She was wearing a mask. She grabbed a pound of ground beef and walked away.

Strangely the bottom round was still $4 dollars a pound. So I bought one. Cooked it in the oven. Three lbs. I will slice it and wrap it in plastic tomorrow. Wrap it in tin foil. Write Taco Meat on it. Put it in the freezer.

I forgot to get corn tortillas. Next time.

Although, I did get a pizza cutter, a ladle, and metal measuring spoons. Which made me feel like a prick. $12 dollar extravagance.

My scheme to be an Anti-Billionaire is not working out very well. I just sit around doing nothing. Money just comes into my bank account. My rent is paid for months in advance. I can just buy whatever I feel like at the grocery store without consequence. I am clean. Healthy. I can do whatever I feel like. As long as it is in my own apartment. I am more productive than ever. A cute cat just looks out the window. Waggin' its' tail. And the cute cat ain't me. Professor Curly showers regularly. G just conks like a log on the couch all day. I got the good life.

Where is Paris Hilton when I need her?

Well, I know where she is. And she gets WAY too much credit for being a tragic figure. She is not tragic. Stupid? Yes. Rich? Yes. Tragic? No.

But maybe the way that Celebrity has taken a hit in the midst of this pandemic is a way to view how the Stock Markets have taken a hit is something to give a closer look at?

I think I might give it some thought.

DAY THIRTY-FOUR

Holy moly! There have been some new developments that will last a lifetime. G moved back home to her mom's. She and Professor Curly had a frank discussion. A short walk to the pharmacy. Followed by an English lunch of cucumber sandwiches and artichoke. Red drink and Diet Coke. Shiver still lives here. For the duration.

Lately my predictions have been a little spot on. I hope the one where the Orange Douche gets on Air Force One and flies to Russia to seek Sanctuary comes true sooner than later.

This nightmare can't end soon enough.

Dinner of a New England Steamer. Chicken Pot Pie and carrots and peas cooked in chicken stock with butter and salt and pepper.

The mail seems to have stopped. My mom's birthday is coming up. Ten days. I am going to send her a card tomorrow. But now I am wondering if it is a good idea. And if the card will ever get there. I guess I should just send it, and hope for the best. But that also seems like a risky way to be thinking at the moment. Professor Curly thinks it will be fine. But she is the same person that ordered a "Cute top for Zooms" via the internet just a week ago.

Everyone is wearing a mask now. Even the cute old man with the tiny poodle. And gloves. Which is great. The world is a better place without more assholes. Not that the cute old man was being an asshole, it's just, fucking hell! let's beat this thing first. Then be an asshole.

Jonny claims we stole his baking pan from Harlem. I don't remember it that way, but then again I never owned a baking pan until I got together with Professor Curly. You do the math. Sorry, Jonny. I would mail it back to you, but, ya know? On a positive note, the cookies I have been baking are fantastic! Hats off!

Speaking of China. China, the same country that has had unprecedented economic growth over the last forty years, the same country that has no qualms killing millions of their own citizens for that growth, shut down their own economy to contain this virus, and now we have assholes in the streets waving swastika flags, and AK-47s around because the country is on a three week hiatus, demanding to get their, Liberties Back? Where do these people work? Are they really that willing to die for the economy? For Wall Street? I wonder if they know that Wall Street is doing just fine. That the precedent that was set during, "Too Big To Fail" meant that from here on out, there is no risk in the Risk/Reward system that we have set up in order to fund big businesses? That there is no longer a Risk in the Risk/Reward system? It is only Reward now? And the only Risk is for the people that work for them? That the current administration has taken a bad policy from the last administration, and just amplified it exponentially?

But I digress. I am going to the ATM tomorrow to take more cash out. Something tells me that when this idiotic bail-out to the 1 percent backfires they will just drain our bank accounts. And as virus-laden money is latently, a dollar in the hand is worth a Kate in the Bush.

If I only could. Make a deal with god. I'd get him to swap our places. I'd be running up that hill. Running up that road. With no problems.

Iron your money.

DAY THIRTY-FIVE

Five weeks. Becca came over. Got Professor Curly drunk. Shiver left. Got caught scratching the Oriental. G colored her hair again. This time with more gusto. Purple. She is in very high spirits. Think she likes the new developments. Taco for lunch. Leftover macaroni and cheese. Spinach. Calzone for dinner. Sauteed broccoli.

Forgot to mention the bonin' yesterday. Bed bonin'. Four day build up. Quite zesty.

Florida can go fuck itself. I think the calamity it is heading towards will be epic. I wonder how they are going to try to hide it from the press. Maybe the thinking is that nobody with an ounce of sense will go down there. Too dangerous. I guess we just have to wait and see.

Had a funny thought today about white flight because of the pandemic. Urban areas won't get less liberal if 25% of the population moves to the suburbs, and back to small towns. But just by numbers alone, rural America will become more liberal. How is that for unintended consequences?

But then what happens when the conservative population gets pushed out of the rural areas, and are forced to move to the city to find jobs and housing? Pandemonium. That's what.

I really hope all the poor people who were offered a larger sum of money for their property than it was worth so some rich white developer could gussy it up and sell it to a rich white family just turn around and come right back to town and buy their homes back. At a lower price. And with all the new construction. I know there is no justice in the world. But that would be the epitome of justice.

That, and if they dug up Robert Moses's grave and skull fucked his corpse.

It looks like we might have successfully flattened the curve in New York. Although, people are still acting like idiots. But if we can hold it together. We might see some progress. Whatever that means. Maybe don't go to Central Park and act like things are back to normal. But that is already happening, so my expectations are not very high. But if we believe in ourselves, and try hard enough, maybe someday soon we can find tortillas in the grocery store again.

Was reading today that these protests about opening the economy prematurely were in order to get Fuddruckers open again. Which is pretty funny. But I feel like the joke would be better served if it was, Cracker Barrel. Who the hell knows what a Fuddruckers is? I mean, I do. But I grew up in Wyoming. We would go to Billings just to eat there. Just thinking about a Fuddruckers makes me want to become vegetarian. Eating a steak in a butcher shop, no thanks. The smell of blood and fat particulates. It's like the dining equivalent of Han Solo cutting that hairy dinosaur open to stay warm. And then sitting down to a tasty hairy dinosaur steak that you just cut from the walls of the carcass. By candle light. But in broad daylight. Surrounded by overweight, unhealthy people.

But since, somehow, this idiotic administration has turned a pandemic into a culture war, people are willing to die for this luxury.

Ya know, my brother Luke gives me way too much credit for leaving home when I did. I was just being shit on. Self preservation. But whenever I go back. I mean. The way that people age. How my family and my family's friends, my mom and her friends, people like Phyllis, who maintain a curiosity about the world, how they are healthy and content, but then I see the people I grew up with. Fat and angry. Aging and scared. I don't know what to think. What horrible lives they must live. It is somebody else's fault. Always. Like the world somehow moved on and they were left there to wallow. With nobody to help them. And, oh, how they worked so hard to get where they are, but some immigrant is coming to take what they hold dear away. But then they walk seven steps from their front porch, get into their car, or truck, drive to work which is seven blocks away, work doing god knows what, drive to the fast food place for lunch, drive back, work a tiny bit more, go home, order a pizza, eat it while watching Fox News, fall asleep on the couch, and then get up and go to bed.

Rinse. Repeat.

And these are the people that are supposedly going to take over the country? With their Fuddruckers rebellion?

They might have guns, but they are more likely to have a heart attack than they are to stand up and fight for what they believe in. Because frankly, they believe in nothing. I said it before, I will say it again:

Republicans are racist liars, who hate the poor, and only care about money.

The last Republican that actually pulled himself up by his bootstraps was John McCain. And he is dead now. Regardless of what the Orange Douche says. And his daughter is a racist liar, who hates the poor, and only cares about money.

But Minnesota just said, Fuck you, you can't ask us to kill ourselves in order to vote. Florida is heading for a reckoning. Michigan will buck. And when the North East is able to open up because we did the right thing, even though it was a disaster for the economy, I don't even know.

I really hope people with money start moving into Worland and start buying up houses. Forcing people to move to Casper or Cheyenne, or god forbid, Denver. I would laugh my ass off.

I feel like Kanye West already started that trend. Cody and! Greybull.

HA HA HA HA

You know, he said he was voting for Trump.

Owning the Libs is one thing, but tying your economic future to a Pyramid Scheme Huckster.

Trump 2020

DAY THIRTY-SIX

Stocks down. Oil prices in the negative for the first time since oil has been a thing. I went to gas up my car today, and they paid ME! Just jokes. It doesn't work that way. I don't own a car. Haven't we been over this before? But crude oil prices are in the negative.

Just saw a very blatant coke deal just go down. My first instinct was to grab some cash, and run down, and stand in line. But the car drove away too fast.

Spent the day dealing with electronic mails. And now I can only blind copy for some reason. I haven't read anything about it, but maybe America On Line has a new policy. I will look into it.

One fried egg. One strip of bacon. One quarter of an apple. And a bowl of oatmeal for breakfast. Lunch was tacos and yesterday's broccoli. The tortillas I am making are starting to get better. The trick, it turns out, is to really rough up the dough. Man handle it. As they used to say. Before men got outlawed. Just jokes. Men were always outlawed, we just never knew it. And now there is an accountability issue that I find pretty hilarious, but I think others find a little frustrating. But then again, I have been pretty bullied in my life, so watching the patriarchy disintegrate gives me shameful joy.

Laundry day. With hilarious results. Three times. Three times! When I was wringing out the laundry I had to take my bathrobe off so I didn't get the sleeves wet. And three times I was wringing out the laundry my long johns pulled down, and exposed half of my butt. And three times! I was able to trick Professor Curly to come into the bathroom to help me only to find me bent over, on my knees, with my naked butt half-exposed. By the third time she was actually pretty annoyed. But the two times before that, pure gold!

Joey!

Now I know how the Boy Who Cried Wolf really felt. As he was being eaten by the wolf. It was worth it!

Dinner of homemade Hot Pockets. Cecina, mushrooms, onion, cheddar. Boiled peas. Mailed the birthday card to my mom. Hopefully it gets there. The usual mailman is back. Thank god he isn't sick like I feared. Still waiting on two letters though. One for me, and one for Professor Curly.

Claimed weekly benefits on UnEmployment Insurance for the third time. No reason to believe I won't get it. Not sure what to do with the money though. I know I will need it in the future, but if by some miracle I can go back to work before the summer is over, and I don't need it, I think I will use it to make care packages for people who are in need. Maybe set up a distribution kiosk in the car port outside the building. Anyone who asks. Foods. Toiletries. Maybe put a $20 dollar bill in each box. Detergent.

Things are going to get really hard. Things are going to stay that way. For a very long time. And it is becoming more and more apparent that the racist liars who hate the poor and only care about money are trying to kill us. The idea of having a Job is over. Thank god. But it means that we are left naked, and flapping in the breeze. No health care. No job security. We are becoming a nation of drug dealers. I am watching it unfold outside my window. The people that have the luxury to stay at home paying people to do their dirty work for them. Paying people to put themselves at risk for their own needs. Billionaires at the heads of corporations who employ people that can work at home who need basic items employing people who can't work at normal jobs to do their bidding for them. Like groceries. Laundry. This pandemic, and the gig economy, just created a new class of citizen: The Indentured.

But there is no way to stop it. It is too late. You can think that Bernie was too far left, and too ambitious with his thinking, but you would be wrong. First of all, he is just barely in the middle of all politics. His ideas land exactly in the middle of what we should be talking about. But since the racist liars who hate the poor and only care about money are so very far to the right, we get gaslit into thinking we have a problem with funding things that make economic sense and would benefit the whole of American life in a much more pragmatic way than their proposals. But that ship has sailed. And we don't have the luxury to experiment at the moment. Because we need to get this fucking maniac out of office. Now! But we have to wait until November.

Close your eyes and think of England.
Bernie 2020
Biden 2020
Wish on an eyelash for Stacey Abrams for VP.

DAY THIRTY-SEVEN

Stocks way down. Oil prices up. Bowery is down. Bronx is up. New York, New York. Not sure what was for breakfast. Professor Curly had eaten before I got up. Not sure why. Lunch of cecina tacos on homemade flour tortillas. Onion, jalapeño, tomato, iceberg lettuce, cheese, squirt of lemon. Rather be a squirter than a blurter. Look with your eyes, not with your mouth.

Another day of fun with electronic mails. While Professor Curly gets nominated for more awards. I feel like this would be my worst nightmare if I was Iver Findlay or Eric Dyer. I say something dumb and can't get out from under it, while my hot sexy girlfriend rakes in the awards that would change my feelings about myself. But she deserves all the attention she is getting. And it is nice to have an honest discussion about uncomfortable things.

Thunderstorms today. Thirty minutes of peace

while they happened. It's nice to get outside of yourself sometimes. I took the moment to scrape the seagull shit off the bedroom window. It was like concrete. I had to use a chisel. A little like washing Professor Curly's underpants last week. Minus the rock hammer.

Frozen pot pie for dinner. Peas and carrots. I made a tasty apple dish with leftover pancake mix, butter, and brown sugar. PeriProsecco. Coca-Cola futures are down. Because people aren't going out to eat for every meal. Also, car crashes are down so much in California that supposedly they are saving something like $80 million dollars a day by not having to deal with them. Add that to the 90% decline in airline travel. Obesity and Climate Change. If you need more proof that we are literally killing ourselves for the sake of the Economy, and Wall Street, well.

I may never go back to work again. Ever. I am going to buy a shovel, and lean it by the front door. And whenever somebody comes by to get money from me, I am going to take that shovel, and start digging. And then I am going to keep digging. And digging. And digging. And eventually I am gonna dig a hole to China. And when the Chinese Government shows up and asks me for my passport, I am going to dig myself back to America. And when I get back to America, and people start showing up to ask me for money, I am going to start digging. And digging. And digging. And eventually I am gonna dig a hole to China.

And there is nothing anyone can do about it.

I am tired. I don't want to work for somebody else anymore. But I also don't want to start a business. There are four businesses open by me. A deli, a coffee shop, a funeral home, and a gas station. The deli is useful. The funeral home won't get my money until I am dead. I have no desire to go to the coffee shop. Even when it wasn't dangerous. And I don't drive. This is what passes for local economy. The disconnect is absurd. Everything is outsourced. The economy is meaningless. We need to embrace this. I never spend money. I hate spending money. If I spend money it means I have to make more money. And I don't want to make more money, because I hate making money. Because work sucks. Working is fine. Digging a hole to China would be a great job for me. But work itself. Getting up because an alarm goes off and then getting on a train. And then travelling for hours. And then doing something that is mostly unpleasant. So you can pay a rent. Or eat a food. I would rather stay at home and eat worms.

However, Society says I need to engage. Which

is fine for other people. But how come everything I contribute to Society doesn't have any real value? How come nobody sent me the memo? I am okay washing dishes for a living as long as I can write in the evenings. But that won't work, because you have to live in a city to do that. And your rent will be too high. So you have to get another job. And that job will be dangerous and scary. And could possibly kill you. Well, that is okay, I guess I could write about that. Yeah, no. It's still just a job. You will have to get up really early, and live in hotel rooms. And the pay won't be as good as it pretends to be. So you will still be tired all the time. And stuck in the suburbs using the tax money that comes from the city. Which you traveled from in order to do the job. Which the school you are working at doesn't understand, and thinks comes from the local economy.

Which is a deli. A funeral home. A coffee shop. And a gas station.

DAY THIRTY-EIGHT

Stocks up. Professor Curly wants soups. Parker put the idea in her mind. Something about muffin tops. We will all be starving soon enough. Enjoy it while it lasts.

My vocal timbre has two volumes now. Silence or yelling. Professor Curly had an extra slice of bacon during breakfast. Then instead of just putting the plate she was eating off of on the counter, as per usual, she scraped it off, and put it in the sink. I yelled at her. Because, usually, I eat the fat from the bacon she doesn't eat. As part of my breakfast. So, not only did she eat more bacon than normal, she deprived me of my own breakfast. She had a very hard time taking me seriously when I was yelling. Smiling. Thank god. But it was very frustrating. I shouldn't have yelled at her though. But like I said. I have only two vocal timbres anymore. Silence or yelling.

Read two articles today that reinforced some thoughts I was having. One was that people are leaving the city in droves. And not coming back.

Breaking leases. Buying houses. Et cetera. The other one is that the French government is now giving nurses and doctors nicotine patches in order to combat the virus. The theory is that nicotine itself is a natural combatant. So here is what we know:

It kills old people more.

It kills black people more.

It helps to smoke, or not smoke, or something.

The drug the Orange Douche said you should take because, "What do you have to lose?" is more likely to kill you than it is to help you.

Everyone should wear a mask in public.

Everyone should wear gloves in public.

Wash your hands.

Stay at home.

America is doing a really shitty job at this. And we are going to be dealing with this crisis for at least a decade. If not longer.

G had a school thing yesterday with the Shoah Foundation. Which I thought sounded very interesting. They deal with the Holocaust. I think Shoah just means Holocaust. But apparently the thing was just a video with a bad sound quality of a woman playing a piano. Which is too bad. But I think school itself, as we know it, is over. And good riddance. I think the idea of 30 kids in a room learning about how Paul Revere did a "Two if by land!" sprint down Daytona Beach riding Seabiscuit and saving us from Ho Chi Minh is a little bunk. I do think that it will mean we, as parents, will need to be a little more involved from here on out, but from the looks of things, we will have plenty of free time. Starting now, and going very far into the future.

The problem with homeschooling though. Is religion. And we need more science in this world. Not less. Not to mention the social aspects of learning. Something scary is brewing. And I don't think we have a solution ready.

Also, feeding the poor. And abuse awareness [just to start with].

We need widespread reform activated immediately. And I don't think we have a plan for that.

But then the woman across the street is dancing naked on her balcony. Which sounds nice, but is actually annoying. People desire too much attention. Celebrity culture has really taken a hit. It was never that interesting in the first place, but to put it in stark contrast to the, "Real World" issues? It is time to stop being polite. It is time to get real.

Move to Oklahoma. I read today that they will give you $10,000 bucks to relocate. Not sure why. But they need professionals. Turn that state blue. That would be nice. If Oklahoma believed in science, I would consider that a victory.

I got another UnEmployment infusion. I am going to the bank tomorrow to take some cash out. What, with Moscow Mitch saying that states should declare bankruptcy and Status Cuomo refusing to give money to undocumented immigrants, something tells me that they will start coming for your money. Soon, and for the rest of your life. I mean, if the Senate Majority leader, and the Governor of New York, which has a Super Majority at the moment, need I remind you, have the same mind about what to do about funds, things are not looking very good for the average worker.

Deficits don't matter when you are handed a bag of money to look over. They matter a great deal when the check comes. And how they overlap is thus:

The only reason that Moscow Mitch is still in power is because Kentucky gets something like $3 dollars back for every $1 dollar it sends to the federal government. And Status Cuomo gets the same thing in reverse, because he keeps property taxes down for the rich. So as long as he doesn't spend any money on things like infrastructure, his people are happy. Meaning the people in the suburbs, the people in Albany. And there aren't any cities in Kentucky. They both are playing politics only. Both are pieces of shit.

I say, empty your bank accounts. It doesn't matter. Just don't close them. The banks are already charging you to use your money to make themselves more money. Let them sweat. Not a single one of us has millions of dollars riding on this mayhem that is, and was, caused by greed. And if you do have money in the game, it is only related to your retirement, your lifetime of work, meant to benefit the system.

We don't need to burn it down. We just need to turn it on its side. It is pretty simple. Take the reins from the stage coach robbery that is happening, and knock the bandit to the ground.

Or sit and spin. On top of the bully in math class's finger because we knew the answer to the question the teacher asked.

Or the video you are waiting to watch.

The metaphors are all mutually inclusive!

DAY THIRTY-NINE

Taco Burgers! Had a dream last night where I was standing in line to order two taco burgers and a medium soda. When it was time for me to order the place got really busy and the guy about to take my order had to go deal with some stuff. When he came back to take my order he forgot I was next in line so he took the order of the person behind me. So I had to get into the back of the line. When I got back to the front it happened again. I stood there staring at him. He ignored me for a long time. Then finally he took my order. I yelled at him. Then some other guy got really mad at me for yelling at him. Then I got mad at that guy, and started yelling at him:

How is it cowardice to stand up for myself! It is just as cowardly for him to ignore me!

Then I spit on the guy.

Taco Burgers for dinner! With tater tots and queso. Yum-yummers!

I have been reading lately that people are microwaving their money. With horrible results.

The money burns. Probably because the dye has metal in it. I said this before. Many times.

Iron your money!

Went to the ATM today. Three mile walk. Came back sweaty, and out of breath. Just joking. Sweaty, yes. Out of breath. No. Was probably the most exercise I have had since the last time I went and took money out of the ATM. Two weeks ago? Nah, four? I don't know. A long time ago. But I guess there is the bonin'. But even that is only like every four days. My point is; I will probably be sore tomorrow.

Stocks are neutral. Bezos went back to work. I am starting to think that I give him too much credit. He might not be the visionary I think he is. I mean, I have mentioned before that I think this pandemic has caught him off guard. I think it has caught most of us off guard. The only people it shouldn't have caught off guard is the fucking Federal Government, but we elected a jackass for a President, and the ruling party, the racist liars who hate the poor and only care about money, were looking at money, and hating the poor, so they were definately caught off guard. It occurs to me that maybe the Orange Douche should have pardoned Bernie Madoff, and put him in charge of the Federal Reserve. At least at that point, we would have a little clarity about what people were thinking. But alas, I digress.

Why has it taken Bezos so long to get back in

charge of his company? Amazon. He knew the pandemic was coming. In the sense that, he sold off billions of dollars of stock before the Stock Market crashed. What has he been thinking in the two months after that happened? Hubris is terminal. I mean, the closest we can get to the Stock Market being connected to the actual economy is Amazon. And guess what happens when people can't go out and buy things anymore? Literally, can't go out. Physically, can't go out? Hate Amazon all you want, but they are the only game in town. What? Are you going to buy groceries from Twitter? Half of America is lazy. The other half is stupid. And there is plenty of overlap.

I guess I just expected more from the guy. I hope he pulls himself together.

Not that I want Jeff Bezos to succeed, it's just that his business is the only thing keeping us together right now. And as much as Walmart seems to be holding itself together, I can see an easy way for Bezos to shoplift the Walmart employees. Living wage. Decent working conditions. Sick leave. Walmart has always been horrible at these things. Amazon too. But the difference is that people have to go to Walmart. Nobody has to go to Amazon. And whether or not Walmart is thinking about having a delivery service like Amazon in the future, I don't know a single person with a Walmart Prime account.

They missed their chance. And not only that, but good fucking riddance.

And truth is, Amazon can be good for small businesses. Small printing presses, for instance. Who can't afford to print their own books. I mean, that is something that didn't exist ten years ago. But think about it this way:

We have four people in charge of America right now:

Donald Trump

Jeff Bezos

Mitch McConnell

Nancy Pelosi

Who would you rather have in charge?

A sociopath that would rather 2.2 million people die as long as the economy is good and he can get re-elected because of it.

A sociopath that wants all the money in the world, but offers a service that can keep society going?

A sociopath that only cares about white Americans, and is willing to destroy America as long as Rich White Americans are still in charge?

A corporate shill that says all the right things about progressiveness but does nothing that helps the average American and ends up facilitating the racist liars who hate the poor and only care about money?

I don't know. Maybe it would be better if Nancy Pelosi was a sociopath? At least the rest of us wouldn't be flapping in the breeze as she does her grandma-in-seclusion routine, trying to figure out what ice cream to eat while the poor are starving to death.

We have power. We are just not using it.

I pick sociopath number two. Jeff Bezos. At least we get food. They say that the reason why Democracy works is because there has never been a famine. And I believe it. On an emotional level. I have starved many times in my life. If I have to choose between a person whose big political gamble is to rip up the papers during a State of the Union speech and a guy who has a factory that employees millions of people and gives me food? I would pick the latter.

However! If Trump and McConnell are still in power at the end of this year. Democracy will get it's first famine.

And it is going to suck.

DAY FORTY

Here's a thought[1]: The last Depression gave birth to Las Vegas, this Depression will kill it.

Stocks up. God knows why. Money really does make money. And like lice, it refuses to die.

Jack told me to watch out for Taco Burglars. That was funny. And true.

Raining all day. Took a lot of energy to get out of bed. Professor Curly never made the bed. But she did take a shower. I could care less if the bed ever got made. But then again I shared a bed with two brothers when I was pretty young, but old enough to remember, and the way you do that is to rotate every night. Two get the bed, one gets the floor. Making the bed never really factored in. I guess if you don't have a bed to make, there is no reason to make the bed.

The cop car that just drove by had an electronic banner that read, "Do your part — Stand 6 feet

---

1. Turns out that I have no spell check. Neither in my writing program, nor my email. Stay in school!

apart". Catchy. The font was bright blue, however, making it nearly impossible to read.

The Orange Douche last night suggested, at a press conference, that you should drink bleach and then shine a flashlight down your throat if you want to kill the virus. Then today he claimed it was a trap for the media to fall into. I hope he follows his own advice.

Pancakes for breakfast. BLTs for lunch. Chicken Pot Pie for dinner. Professor Curly says she can't keep going at this rate. The new joke is that she is gaining the Covid 19. I guess like the freshman 15. Like, from college. But it is a little much. How much I have been cooking, and how much she has been eating. We are starting a new regime tomorrow. She cooks her own breakfast. I make her a light lunch. Then dinner can be whatever. I told her not to worry so much. We will all be eating nothing but beans soon enough. But, whatever. I have probably a gallon of bacon grease in the freezer. For when those times come.

I did an experiment today to see if I could induce panic in my body. It didn't work. I seem to have lost my sense of fear and dread. Which has happened before. And I remember this because I always have the same thought whenever it happens. Agatha Christie and Kurt Vonnegut Jr.

From **Murder At The Vicarage**: I guess I will just resign myself to being uncomfortable, and having terrible things to eat.

From a KVJR book I don't recall the name of: When I learned that Joseph Heller slept in a fetal position most of his life, and then one day switched to sleeping flat on his back, like a corpse, that really bummed me out.

I am paraphrasing, of course. But at this point? Every ten years, a disaster that supposedly we are incapable of preparing ourselves for? I don't buy it. I am resigned to it. I am thinking of having a shirt printed that reads:

Corona Livin'

It should have palm trees on it, but I have never figured out how to do that. If you recall:

Bikini Atoll: Birthplace Of The Bomb

With two palm trees pointing in opposite directions, and a nuclear bomb exploding in the middle. But I can't draw for shit.

Tom sent me a book about Pyramids. Which is awesome. The Post Office put it in a plastic bag because it was falling apart in transit. The package. The return address says Brooklyn, but the stamps are George Herbert Walker Bush, which suggest that he is still in St. Louis. Always the optimist. Hate to break it to you, Tom. You live in St. Louis now. We ALL live in St. Louis now. Golden Arches To The West! The Gateway Belt.

Michael from Um, the band I am in, his wife's dad just died from the Coronavirus. I don't have any details aside from those, but it is scary. And close. And serious. I really wish the federal government was taking this more seriously. I mean, America has over 50,000 deaths from this. 25% of the global deaths reported. Georgia opening up again, for no fucking reason. Michigan protests that are certain to increase the death count. And the numbers are still going up. Daily! We haven't even peaked. By sheer numbers alone, we will have nearly 150,000 American deaths by the end of May! If. IF! We can curb it now. Which we are not doing. If you are older, or compromised, stay home! It is not worth it to go out!

And also! New York reported the lowest daily death rate since April 1st. Twenty-three days ago. So those numbers are not coming from us anymore. We just might have a nice spring after all. Apple blossoms and everything. That is until the white panic that fled to the countryside realizes there are no hospitals out there, and panics back into the city, starting the chain of death all over again.

Chaucer.

DAY FORTY-ONE

G came back. For the night. No Shiver. Chicken tacos for dinner. Homemade flour tortillas. Fried potatoes. Think I finally figured out the potatoes. The tortillas too, but still need to do another round of those before I am sure.

  Fried Potatoes:
    3 medium sized russet potatoes
    3 tbsp canola oil
    kosher salt
    large nonstick frying pan
    spatula
    peeler
    knife
    cutting board

  Wash potatoes. Peel. Cut in half, lengthwise. Cut halves in half, lengthwise. Cube. Put frying pan on stove. Medium heat. Pour half of oil in frying pan. Heat until shimmering. Add potatoes. Pour remaining oil on top. Stir with spatula. 3 tbsp of oil is approximate. The potatoes should be coated, but not frying in a pool of oil. Butter won't work. It has a low burning point. Olive oil also won't work. For the same reason. If you can't follow that direction. Stop reading now, and politely go suck an egg.

The trick to frying potatoes is simple. Fry the potatoes only. My instincts have always been to add other things when cooking. Like onions. Or garlic. My instincts were, and are, wrong. Potatoes are a nasty beast. Or more specifically, a specific beast. They are starchy, and uniform. Moist, but not wet. They need to be cooked thoroughly. Reverse pasta. Instead of cooking by letting the water in, they cook by letting the water out.

Cook slowly, stirring often. The reason a spatula is the best tool for this is thus: The potato has a memory. It wants to stay together. With itself. Treat the cubes like a crowd. Don't single the cubes out. I have a bendy plastic spatula that I use when cooking in the nonstick frying pan. Which is good for turning over, and shoving the potatoes around with the front edge. Scraping the bottom of the frying pan.

I can't tell you how long to cook them. Golden brown is what I went with. But it was more like a light golden brown. They will be slightly crispy on the outside, and almost mashy in the middle. I think you should allow for at least thirty minutes of cooking. It could have been more. For me. It might have been an hour. Time is meaningless right now.

Sprinkle salt on them when finished.

Becca came by. With Amanda. Our neighbor,

for some reason, decided to bring out a speaker, and blare Christian tunes, making it almost impossible to talk. Professor Curly went down. I said hi out the window. It was too loud. I could hear them talking at the back of the apartment. In order to compensate. Something about a trick to end social distancing. Which sounded like a pyramid scheme. I can hang out with one friend. Then I have to wait for two weeks. Then I hang out with two friends, and they hang out with two friends. Then we all wait for two weeks. Then we all hang out with six friends, and wait for two weeks. Ad nausea.

Wish I had more feelings about hanging out with people. But I don't. Even my desire to drink beer has taken a hit. I still feel like drinking a few beers when I tickle the ivories, but the act itself is becoming exhausting. Going to the deli. The grocery. The recycling. The bathroom breaks. If I do the math, I have probably dropped my intake by 15%, maybe more, if I include the emotional decline in desire. These are dark times.

I really thought the Orange Douche would resign today. I mean, why not? At this point it would be a lateral move. He won't be prosecuted. There is no way he can win the argument that he did a good job with the pandemic. The economy is doomed for at least ten years. I mean, what does he have to lose? To echo his catch phrase. It would send the Republican party into chaos. He would still be the hero to his base. Pence would take all the blame. The Republican party could pretend like nothing happened, and bring back Mitt Romney. Which would give something for The Orange Douche to rail against. It's a win-win-win. Instead of giving the double V for victory signs when he gets onto Marine One he could just smile and shrug. Saying:

Ain't I a stinker?

The press would eat it up. We are still very much in a crisis. Plus, he is enough of a piece of shit as to do it. Who knows. Maybe he will embrace all the DNC talking points, and run on the Democrat ticket in November. Maybe even absorb all the Bernie talking points. Run as a third party populist. Blame the Republican party for all the problems in America. Nobody will see it coming. Then he will lead us into the Bright Globalist Future that we need to embrace right now before billions of people die from a Nationalist induced plague and famine.

But what do I know? A man can dream still, right?

Bernie 2020-> Biden 2020-> Trump 2020 [R]-> Biden 2020-> Bernie 2020-> Trump 2020 [I]

I said it before, and I will say it again:

If Trump did literally the exact opposite of everything he does, he would be a better President than Lincoln.

DAY FORTY-TWO

Six weeks. Sunday. April 26th. G left. Rain. Salads for lunch. Me, and Professor Curly. Mushrooms. Cucumber. Chicken. Carrot. Tomato. Avocado. White onion. [PC insisted on red onion, but it was too late.] Romaine lettuce. Bacon crisps sprinkled on top. Oil, and vinegar dressing. With smoked paprika. G had a taco. Two tacos. And Mimi's Famous Australian Lunch Tubers. Just joking. About the name. But G's Mimi sent me a recipe for fried potatoes. Very tasty. Kind of similar to last night's potatoes, except smaller, and quicker, and you use extra virgin olive oil. And better potatoes.

Made flour tortillas. Third time is the charm. Or, more like, third time using the same recipe with same results, is the charm.

Torts:
Still not exactly sure what the science is. Specifically. That make these tortillas more successful versus the other recipes I tried. Baking powder, maybe? Maybe because I paid more attention to the amount of water I was using?

Maybe it was because I used two types of fat? Or that I brought the dough in wet, and then pulled it back dry? Or that I used the counter top, and not the cutting board when I rolled them out? Maybe it was because I kneaded the dough in the bowl the first time? Or that I let the dough sit for an hour, and then put it in the fridge for another hour? Maybe it was because the skillet I used to cook them was at the perfect heat? There are a lot of unknowns.

1 1/2 tsp baking powder [not baking soda]
2 tsp table salt
3 tbsp vegetable shortening [Crisco]
3 tbsp lard
4 cups flour [all purpose]
1 1/2 cups warm water
rolling pin
large bowl [like really large, mixing bowl, punch bowl size]
medium bowl [the size of the ball of dough]
counter top [something with a design you can discern through a thin layer of dough]
plastic wrap
large cast iron skillet
large knife
dish towel

Put flour into the large bowl. This isn't baking, so there is no need to be exact, but I did scoop the flour into the measuring cup, and leveled off with the back of a butter knife. Add baking powder, salt, vegetable shortening, and lard. Mix with one of your hands. The mixture will become kind of grainy but soft. Don't squeeze the batter together. I guess. I didn't. Not sure if that matters.

With your other hand, slowly add the water. One thing I know I was doing wrong before was adding all the water regardless. New York is humid. And at sea level. The 1 1/2 cups of water is kind of just a suggestion. I would imagine that in Wyoming, in April, at 5,000 feet, you probably will need that much water. But what do I know? I don't live there. Did you put lip balm on today? I didn't.

Mix the water in slowly. There will be a point when the dough seems like it is too sticky, but you are out of dry flour. This is called, Coming In Wet. Which is good. Bring the dough to that point. Then add sprinkles of dry flour until the ball of dough can be squeezed without sticking to your hands. This is called, Bringing It Back Dry.

Knead the dough in the bowl for ten minutes or so. It should honestly feel like Play-Doh.

Then remove the ball of dough, and walk around the apartment squishing it between your fingers. Then making a ball. Then punching it with your fist. Then take it over to Professor Curly, and mold it into a ball, and hold it next to her face, and say, Oh, I thought this was you, but you got a tan. Then run away.

She is a beautiful alabaster princess.

Put the ball of dough into the smaller bowl, and cover with plastic wrap. Let sit for an hour. Clean up. Do the dishes. Clean the countertops. Thoroughly. Take this time to soak your cast iron skillet. With dish soap. You don't need to use a cast iron skillet, I don't think. Maybe you just have a large frying pan? Whatever it is, it should be as clean as you can get it. Something with a consistent surface. That can maintain heat.

After an hour has passed, remove the ball of dough from the bowl, and knead again. This time on the counter top. As well as in your hands. Make a round ball, then smash it down, then make a round ball, then smash it down. Do this for ten minutes. Put back in the bowl. Cover with the plastic wrap. Put in the fridge.

Let sit until you are ready to make the torts. At least an hour.

If you are not really in the mood to finish this recipe, you can put the dough in the freezer. Simply put it in a plastic bag. Spin it. Then put in the freezer. When you get into the mood, remove from the freezer, and let thaw.

If you are in the mood to finish the recipe, remove from the fridge and knead the dough one last time. Another ten minutes. But first, place the cast iron skillet on the stove top, and put the heat at just under medium. Make sure the skillet is clean. Very, very clean. And don't rush. The pan needs to be at equilibrium. Neither coming nor going. Heat wise.

When the dough has been through the third kneading, roll into a ball. Place onto countertop. Cut in half. Roll each half into a ball again. Then each half into a ball again. Repeat. You should end up with 16 balls of dough, about the size of a golf ball. If you know what the size of a golf ball is. Bigger than a meatball, smaller than a cue ball. I don't even know. Just cut the thing into 16 equal sizes.

Roll each ball into a ball of its own. Set to the side.

Here is the tricky part. Very frustrating at first, but gets kind of zen the more you do this. In order to make round tortillas you need to be very patient. Roll the balls into a ball, then kind of flatten into a disk. Put on the counter top. Then roll in one direction. Just once. Turn the dough perpendicular. Then roll in one direction. Just once. Repeat. Then repeat again. Then keep repeating.

Every time you do this the dough will shrink back. But it will also keep getting larger. Roll. Peel up. Turn. Roll again. Peel up. Turn. Eventually you will have a circle resembling a tortilla. Keep at it. You will know that the tortilla is ready to cook when you can see the countertop through the dough. Translucent. But not so translucent that there are holes in the dough.

When you are ready to cook the first tort, take the dish towel, and find a flat surface. Lay the dish towel flat.

Peel the raw tortilla from the counter top, and drape onto the skillet. There should be a sizzling sound. The dough should start to bubble. Flip quickly after that. There should be brown spots. This time the tortilla should start to balloon. Let sit for just seconds. Flip again. Let sit for even less seconds. Remove, and put on top of the dish towel. Cover.

Note* It is better to undercook than to overcook the first time you are cooking. You will reheat them. Which will cook them again.

Repeat this process. It is best to just do one tortilla at a time. The instinct is to rush it. That instinct is wrong. You don't want to be busy rolling out a tort while your other tort burns. There is no point to that.

I, personally, would cook only half of this recipe at a time. I do an 8×8 method. Eight out, Eight in. Why did the lesbian read so many menus? Because she ate out.

Freeze the other half.

One more thing to note. The torts get pretty steamy. It is best to rotate them within the dish towel. Flip them over. Shuffle them. That way they won't get soggy. Then, if you have a plastic bag, put them in the plastic bag. For later. Or, just eat them ASAP.

With beans. Or ground beef. Or cecina. Or chicken. Or et cetera.

Richard Hake died. That makes me very sad. Rest in peace. My feelings about WNYC are very complicated, but he was a good one. Brian Lehrer should be mayor of New York.

On a lighter note. The showboat babe across the street has started doing naked yoga in front of her window. She really has too much time on her hands. I hope she figures it out.

DAY FORTY-THREE

They canceled the New York Primary. Stocks up. I can't believe it. I really can't. They didn't even lie about it. They said they wanted to reduce turnout for the election. The DNC. I can't remember the last time I felt this frustrated. And mind you, I have been stuck inside for forty-three days now. Which is something I can laugh about. This is much different. I knew they were thinking about it. I just didn't think they would be stupid enough to do it. They just signed us up for the Jelly of the Month Club. The thing that led Cousin Eddie to kidnap Clark W. Griswald's boss, leading his wife to describe Cousin Eddie as, A big, beastly, bulging man.

"That has effectively ended the real contest for the Presidential nomination," Kellner said. "And what the Sanders supporters want is essentially a beauty contest that, given the situation with the public health emergency that exists now, seems to be unnecessary and, indeed, frivolous."

They are daring progressives to vote for Trump.

Scott thinks it is because they want someone to blame when we inevitably lose the election in November. I think it is stupider than that. I think that they think that we will just fall in line. We have no choice. Which I think is the reason that New York holds its primary so late anyway. It worked in 2016. Can you imagine if New York and California voted at the same time in the primary? If Bernie won both California and New York at the same time? See what I mean about stupid? How are we so stupid with politics on the left?

Say what you want about "Bernard Brothers"; they may, or may not exist. If they do, it is on Twitter, and the Joe Rogan show. But half, 50% at least, of the Democratic party is progressive. My guess is that it is way more than that, but Americans tend to try their hardest to ignore politics. But whatever. I won't let you drag me down that hole, Joey! No matter how hard you try.

My point is, what message are you sending to half of your constituency by cancelling a vote? Especially now. When we need to figure out mail-in voting?

It beggars sense. [This is not over]

Lunch was tuna sandwiches, and salad. Cherry Coke.

Did some bonin'. With hilarious results. I was reading Professor Curly's menu to completion, and then switched to a dog move. Looked over.

Two men on a balcony doing construction. Not sure what they saw. But probably everything. Had to drop and roll. Very sophisticated. And complicated. Same results. But, it's the journey, right?

Speaking of results. Did a good pasta for once. Very complicated, but I got really worked up today after they cancelled the election. I downloaded an absentee ballot request. Filled it out. Mailed it. I am voting for Bernie before I vote for Biden in the general election. Even if it means writing his name on a piece of dog shit, and shoving it down Douglass Kelner's throat, which is currently sucking Tom Perez's dick [this is not over].

But after the bonin', and the body shock of frustration from the cancelled primary, I needed to relax. So I put on a little Jackson Browne, and hit the sauce. Pans, that is. I hit the saucepans.

Just joking about the Jackson Browne. There is nothing at the moment in my daily routine that would allow for an extended Jackson Browne session. I'm not an ostrich.

I put on a little David Pakman, and started cooking dinner. I knew I was going to fry some chicken. I wanted to make a rice dish. But we don't have any rice. And I personally don't like rice enough to risk a dangerous run to the grocery store to get it. Lord knows Professor Curly wasn't going out. She is a rake at this point. I am surprised she only asks for three foot rubs a day now. But she has switched from throwing quarters at me while I do it, to throwing dollar bills. Which is easier on my ears. To be honest.

Beans or pasta. Fried chicken and pasta seemed like a better combo. I was right. Here is the pasta dish:

Pasta Absentee:
    1 medium sized red onion
    1/2 bulb garlic
    6 white mushrooms
    6 baby carrots
    2 tbsp of butter
    1 cup milk
    kosher salt
    1/2 package dried spaghetti
    small frying pan
    large frying pan
    medium pot
    large pot for cooking pasta [with lid]
    knife
    cutting board
    tongs
    2 colanders [one for the pasta, one to strain]
    wooden spoon

The idea for this dish was a way to kill time, and to not think too much.

Make the stock.

The nice thing about stocks is that you can cook them for the entire day, and they just get better with time. And they smell good. But you don't have to cook them all day. In fact, I think they are ready to be used about an hour after they come to a boil, and you have reduced them to a simmer.

Cut both ends off the onion. Peel the outer layer off. Including the skin. Cut into four rings. Fill the medium-sized pot 3/4's the way full with water. Put the onion rings in. Turn the heat to high.

Throw mushrooms and carrots in. Butter. Cut the stem ends off the garlic. Peel, and add to stock. Sprinkle some kosher salt. Bring to a boil.

When boiling, reduce heat to a simmer.

After about an hour, remove the mushrooms with the tongs. Set to the side. Put them on the cutting board if you want. That is where they will end up anyway.

Fill up large pot with water. 3/4's full. Put on stove. Cover. Turn heat to high. Bring to boil.

When boiling add spaghetti. Cook until just south of al dente. A double tooth. Doppio dente. If you don't know pasta this is hard to gauge. But it should feel like you should cook the pasta for one more minute when you test to see if it is done. Pour into colander in sink. And run cold water over. Stopping the cooking process.

Leave the pasta alone.

I have two colanders. One for pasta, and one for other things. Mesh. Hand held. You really don't need either of these if you have a large bowl, and a pair of tongs. But if you don't have any of these things, I don't know what to say. Get these things. Or don't. But it is going to make this next step kind of hard.

Place the large frying pan on top of the stove. Take your mesh colander, and strain the stock over the large frying pan. Turn the heat to medium. Reduce the stock.

Meanwhile. Chop up the mushrooms. Almost minced. Add to small frying pan. Place on stove. Turn on heat. The same heat as the stock. Medium. Add the milk. When the stock, and the milk/

mushroom mix seem to be simmering at the same rate, add the milk/mushroom mix to the stock. Reduce until there is about 1/8 of an inch of liquid in the large frying pan. Turn off heat.

Move the reduction to a place without any heat. I had to use a stool, but maybe you have more counter space, or a larger stove top. Add the pasta to the reduction. Mix with tongs. Coating all the pasta. With the reduction. Put the frying pan back on the stove. Turn on a very low heat. The 2 setting, if it is electric. Slowly bring to temperature. This took about fifteen minutes for me. Don't rush it. The pasta still needs to cook, but just a little, and you don't want to bring it to temperature before you allow the pasta to absorb the sauce.

Serve in a large bowl. With garlic bread, and peas. And fried chicken. And beer.

[This is not over]

DAY FORTY-FOUR

Stocks down. Three yard stare has set in. I find myself just staring into space. Not looking at anything. Thinking about anything. Kind of relaxing. Another installment of UnEmployment benefits. 58,000 deaths in America. From the virus. More reports of people drinking bleach to cure the virus. The President is a jackass.

Started to grow an avocado from seed. Won't know if it will be successful for a couple weeks.

Moved the Christmas tree into the ante-room. Moved the shelves into the living room. Hung from the wall. Now with books. Started a pretty big fight. About personal space. Dissolved pretty quick. Mostly about unexpected sadness. Balance in relationships. Turns out it is more embarrassing to be caught fighting by two guys doing construction outside an open window, than it is to get caught bonin'. Between that, and the three yard stare, it is official. We live in a fish bowl. [it's O'-fish-bowl]

Tacos Guggenheim for dinner. With sauteed broccoli. PeriProsecco.

Flavoring a bone-in piece of pork for tomorrow. 4 pounds. Not really sure what the plan is. Cook it until it is done. Maybe carnitas? Also, got some cow feet to make stock. Tomorrow will be fun.

Grocery is out of flour. Which is more funny than anything. It's like when everyone got an iPhone, and suddenly became a photographer. But with flour, and bread, and death. But also, there is no shortage of whole wheat flour. If that tells you anything.

Unrelated. Bought a bag of whole wheat flour. Not sure how to use it. But will find out soon enough.

They are also out of cornstarch. Which confuses me. When do you ever use that? For gravy, I suppose. I was going to use it to make General Tso's Chicken. I bought a bag of corn flour. Doubt it is the same. But I think it means I can make tamales! I suppose I will need corn husks, but that is for Ron. Later Ron.

More anecdotal evidence that smokers fare better. Which is funny. Because in the beginning, the reason why men were dying more than women is because men smoked more. And because smokers touched their faces more. And were more likely to get it. By funny, I mean, idiotic. Maybe newspapers shouldn't publish anecdotal "Evidence" one way or the other. Or the Orange Douche shouldn't tell people to drink bleach, and then swallow a flashlight.

This is capitalism at work. Not a free press. Anything to sell newspapers is not a free press. It is an idiotic press acting irresponsibly. The same way it is an idiotic press acting irresponsibly airing the Orange Douche's press briefings live. Even with fact checks in real time.

Damn it! Meant to call James today. Tomorrow. It is Peg Leg's birthday tomorrow. I should call Luke, too. Hump day.

Think I will watch Repo Man tonight. Something about Taco Bell being the only restaurant in the future. Reminds me of Amazon. I really am starting to think Jeff Bezos is an idiot. The same way the Orange Douche is an idiot. Just greed all the way to the bone. It is one thing to want a bunch of money. To make choices based on a desire to have more money. It is an entirely different thing to want ALL of the money. Corruption on a larger scale is still corruption. When Michael Bloomberg was mayor of NYC, it's not like he was too rich to be corrupted by special interest, it's just the special interest was on a larger scale. But Bloomberg only wants some of the money. The Orange Douche is the kind of guy that would pick up a kid, half his size, and move him to the side so he could cut in line, and get his ice cream sundae faster at an ice cream truck.

Jeff Bezos would do the same. Except he would hire someone to do it for him while waiting in the limousine.

Broken clocks. Twice a day. Severely broken humans. Don't use clocks.

Ten rolls of toilet paper left. Half way. I am impressed. We should have been doing this the whole time. Ten rolls over forty-four days? I really swear. Not because I want to give Professor Curly the grief. But I swear. We would go through a roll every two days. And I don't think she is saving swipes. Her yow-yow, and her, bedow-yow, seem very clean. I am thinking that maybe Urban Meadows has been selling us a bill of goods for quite some time now. Do the math:

$44/10 = .22$ per day.

That means that one roll lasts us just over five days! That is double-time! Including G coming over! And the incident with the under-cooked chicken!

I think it may be time to sue. Class Action.

Urban Meadows! You let my butt down! You let Democracy's butt down! In fact! You let the American people's butt's down!

We demand satisfaction!

DAY FORTY-FIVE

Stocks way up. On news of a loss of 5% GDP, and 60,000 deaths in America from the Coronavirus. The disparity is astounding. My guess is that tomorrow when the new jobs numbers come out, we will see a rally like nothing before in the history of the stock market. I think that is tomorrow. Might be Friday. Either way.

I think if there is a breaker for when stocks go into free-fall, there should also be one when they do the opposite. It's only fair. If the system is safeguarded from people losing their shirt in a single day, it should also be safeguarded against people turning their shirt into a tuxedo in a single day.

But what do I know? 40 million people out of work, can't pay rent, no health insurance, can't go back to work because it will kill them, can't collect UnEmployment insurance benefits because America wants them to die.

Tragedy versus statistics. Right? Stalin-style. And the more the right talks about the Economy versus the Health of the American public, it makes me ill. It tinges like Nazi Germany doing experiments on Jewish prisoners in Auschwitz. And their Euthanasia programs. On their own fucking people! Useless feeders. They called them.

But for Fuddruckers. Say what you will about the National Socialists, at least they had an ethos [Walter, ***The Big Lebowski***].

I don't get it. I don't know why we stand for it. I don't understand why there isn't rioting [well, not physical rioting, at the moment, but from the way the newspapers tell it, everything is cherry sundaes]. Rent strikes. Debt strikes. Work strikes. Tax strikes. We are losing the war! We will come out of this in tatters if we don't do something now! They are getting stronger. We are getting weaker.

The plane is crashing! The Pilot is huffing gas. The co-pilot is frantically perusing the owners manual to figure out what all these flashing lights mean!

We need sweeping reform. Now! Not bailouts for billionaires, and their businesses. We need infrastructure. We need public health. Wage increases. Housing security.

One good accident that is happening is that a lot of people getting UnEmployment benefits are making a significant amount of money more from them than they are from being at work. Which hopefully is a wake-up call to a generation of workers that has been gaslit into thinking that the reason they are poor is because they are lazy. If you can work 40+ hours a week working for McDonalds, and only bring in $400 dollars, but you can sit around doing nothing, and bring in $1,000 dollars, what does that say about the equality in the system?

If it is true that we could all just be millionaires, that America has that much money, but the way the system is set up, most of us make $40,000 dollars a year, and the people who are lucky enough to be on top make hundreds of millions of dollars a year, doing the same job, but in a suit. I don't know. I would be pissed. But I am pissed. Been pissed for quite some time. Meet me at Bushwick Avenue and Moffat Street. Any day of the week. I have a pamphlet you can read.

I digress. It has been a peculiar day. Shot a video with Jess, and Emily, and Professor Curly. I had one line:

"She'll never learn. She doesn't have it, mon ami!"

I was holding a cucumber that I played like a flute. A mustache, and a beret. I was supposed to say, Mon ami, like how you would say, Edamame, not sure if I did a good job or not. Post-production. It all happened via computers. So futuristic!

The carnitas turned out well. Although I should have done more research. I cooked the thing for six hours. At 200F. That wasn't long enough. I was afraid I was going to dry the thing out. I cut the choice meats out in time for dinner. The rest is still cooking.

Served the carnitas with a pickled slaw. Including jalapeños. Mimi's potatoes. Corn tortillas. PeriProsecco.

The cow feet didn't do the job I was hoping they would do. I kept getting smells from them that reminded me of when my dad would boil animal heads when I was a teenager. Not very appetizing. But Professor Curly isn't familiar with that smell. So it worked out okay. I am boiling the bone from the pork butt at the moment. So, maybe not all is lost. A stock is a stock.

After watching **Repo Man** last night [which I don't remember as well as I thought I would, and Emilio Esteves is great, but he should yell more] I watched four short videos with Temple Grandin taking us through a meat processing plant. Amazing. All the more reason we should listen to Greta Thunberg. Suffering is obvious, and real. And simple. There are pragmatic steps we can take, right now, that transcend politics. We might all be destined for the slaughter house, but it doesn't need to suck all the way to the shoot.

But who knows? Professor Curly got the virus again. Fourth time? She took a nap today. From 230p-4p. God bless her. I read the bible next to the bed. Praying. The construction guys are nearly finished with their project. Shelving. Stained shelving. They didn't know Professor Curly was dying. In fact, the wife came out at one point to check out the progress. And the daughter. They didn't inquire about the status of Professor Curly. Heartless.

Peg Leg's birthday. She said she would call, but she had phone meetings all day. Try again tomorrow. Didn't call James or Luke. Think Charley must be in Alaska. Or he would have responded to me giving him sass by now. Jack is in his Basement of Dreams. Ilan has DMT vapes.

Murphey is still in Philly. Margy is in Connecticut. Frying pots. Elisabeth is in Norway. Jeff, and Jenny, and Guy, and Luke are all in Colorado. Nate is in Montana. Phyllis is in Worland, I think. Sanae is in California. Jonny is in Harlem. Miette, and Scott, and Grit are in Vermont. Dianne is in MassHole. Becca is in Bushwick. Jess is in Bushwick. Professor Curly is in Bushwick. Brother Luke is in Portland, Maine. Jacob is in Seattle. Tom is in St. Louis. Rambona is in Fort Greene, BK. Peter is on the Upper West Side. Meg is in Ten Sleep, Wyoming. Brian is in Casper, Wyoming.

The list is too long!

"I can't go on. The sunshine hurts my eyes."
-Kate Valk, ***To You, The Birdie***

My point is:

"Be excellent to each other."
-Bill S. Preston, Esq.

Grandin 2020

DAY FORTY-SIX

Turns out you can just grab-em by the pussy. Which means that the old chestnut about how you are always running against the last campaign, is, in this case, exactly true. But in Biden's defense, how can you really tell if someone is DTF?

Professor Curly has gone bongo. She just locked herself in the bedroom, and is singing along to the new Fiona Apple album. Very cute. Voice like an angel. Kind of. In spirit, I guess.

Stocks down. 30 million Americans now on UE or applying for UE. They are reporting that Wall Street has had the best month since forty years ago. Whatever that means. Maybe the Fed pumping $2.5 trillion dollars into the market might have something to do with it? But since I never paid attention to the stock market before this most recent crisis, what do I know? But it does seem a little disingenuous. A Confidence game.

Salad for lunch. Slim pickins' on chicken at the grocery lately. Probably because the workers in the meatpacking are sick, and dying, and are forced by direct order to get back to work, by the Orange Douche. They might be having some problems. My guess about that is that he is worried about getting his cheeseburgers. He doesn't need to worry about the Coronavirus, because he is the President, so PPE doesn't really make a difference to him, but if we run out of meat, we run out of cheeseburgers! It's 1 to 1.

Chinese Steamer for dinner. Steamed broccoli. Minute rice. Boiled potatoes. Fried chicken fingers. Aside from the boiled potatoes, that is what Professor Curly orders from the Chinese take-out, when she used to order from the Chinese take-out. Back before this all began.

With soy sauce.

I really don't want things to go back to the way they were before. This is starting to feel like a vacation. Not in the, I am having a blast in Wyoming, and I don't want to go back to the Rotten Apple, but more like, I went to the Bahamas, and I don't like the beach, and I am spending too much money, money I don't have, but I hate my job so much, I never want to go back, but I have all this debt now, so I have to go back, so I better try and enjoy it while I can, vacation.

I really hope we are collectively learning a lesson. I know we are stupid, us Americans, so we don't learn lessons, but I do hope.

Biden marched on the White House today to

demand that the President put the flag at half-staff in honor of the front-line workers. Which is something. I guess.

Here is the problem with Biden. He did it. Everybody knows it. And it is despicable. And it speaks to the larger problem of sexism in America, and the culture of the Patriarchy. But because we, meaning the Democrats, the DNC, Corporate Media, were so scared of Bernie Sanders getting the nomination, we collectively ignored it. So instead of sussing it out during the primary, we are now in this horrible position of giving the Republicans, the racist liars who hate the poor and only care about money, the same party that elected a serial rapist to the presidency, we are giving them the ability to define the narrative.

We, all of us, are now hypocrites. With a double standard. And it is true. A little nuanced, but true. Biden didn't get a girl drunk, and then lock her in a room with his buddy, and try to rape her, like Brett Kavanaugh, but he did think some broad was hot on his twinky, and giving him the vibe, so much so that he thought it was appropriate to push her against a wall, and penetrate her vagina with his fingers.

Does that mean he should be disqualified to become President? Yes. Does that mean Brett Kavanaugh should not be on the Supreme Court for life? Yes.

Will sexism prevail? Yes. Would we have this

problem if Bernie Sanders was the presumptive nominee? No. We would have different problems. Actual conversations about the state of America, and how to sell them to the American public. But we wouldn't be dealing with sensational politics. Not now. And not for the next six months.

But we dug our grave. We must lie in it.

How do we swallow the hypocrisy? We don't. We plug our noses. Status Cuomo just called the homeless disgusting for living on the subway. Refusing to tax the rich to pay for basic services for people without homes. Do you really want him to be the next President? Not only is he a middle of the road Democrat, but he is also deeply unpopular with anyone aside from the suburban whites, and the very wealthy.

And there is new news coming in that Hilary is waiting in the wings for a second go at it. I can't think of anything more stupider than nominating Hilary Clinton to be the next President. Well, maybe cancelling the New York primaries. That would be pretty stupid. Thank god they aren't doing that.

If we don't plug our noses, we are going to lose!

Tara Reade is going to go on Fox. And it will be a sensation. The media will amplify it until their throats are raw with screaming.

Biden will have to apologize. Stacey Abrams will have to backtrack. Tarnishing her nascent career. The DNC will throw her under the bus.

Meaning, none of the other female candidates will be willing to take a fall. Which leaves us with Warren, who is political kryptonite if we are running a campaign of sensationalism, which it seems like we are.

Times are dark.

The Orange Douche is dropping in polls. But for how long? Things are going to get insanely bad. Pure chaos bad. And as much as the Orange Douche lies every time he opens his mouth, or because the Orange Douche lies every time he opens his mouth, he will always say the right thing. And even though those things he is saying are lies, the media will amplify them.

Rapist One, or Rapist Two? Billionaire Businessman, or Just The Tip Joe?

I mean, I know there is a big difference. The fate of the world as we know it is on trial. Between the Senate, Ruth Bader Ginsburg, immigration, working people, poor people, anyone of color, sexual orientation, the economy, quality of life, et cetera. But if the Right can convincingly convince anyone about bullshit, it is this Right, and this administration. They have done it for forty years now. They have gotten pretty good at it.

Rapist One, or Rapist Two. Billionaire Businessman, or Just The Tip Joe?

I may be wrong. Politics is cheap. I live in NYC. But this is an All Hands On Deck! Haul Ass! Haul Ass! I Think He Went Overboard!, situation.

Fingers crossed.

Biden/Warren 2020

PS. Sanae lives in Oregon, not LA. Charley is in Ten Sleep, not Alaska. Sorry for the confusion.

DAY FORTY-SEVEN

MAYDAY. G is over. Was supposed to come tomorrow, but her school is doing a social distancing plant sale on her stoop in Clinton Hill. Details unclear.

Stocks way down. There is proof that Florida is covering up the number of Virus deaths. Including not counting people whose primary address is not in Florida. Like that makes a difference. If this thing doesn't actually kill America, I think there will be a lot of people in jail for things they are doing right now. Including Ron Desantis.

Talked to Peg Leg and Phylis last night. Things seem pretty chill in Wyoming. Nothing to report. My mom's new coffee machine is really complicated. I have been using the wrong electronic mail for Phylis. For weeks now. Whoever [xxxxxxx]@hotmail.com is, I may never know. But she ain't said shit.

Tuna for lunch. Tacos for dinner. My stock got stinky. The broccoli stems didn't help. Soaking some pintos for tomorrow. Maybe the stock will be a magic ingredient. That, or maybe I ruin a whole batch of beans. Sometimes you got to take risks. God didn't put us on this earth to be safe.

Speaking of idiots. The Fuddrucker Rebellion is gaining more steam. You know, I wonder. What would happen if a bunch of black people showed up with automatic rifles at the Michigan State House? Demanding their freedoms. I think the last time it happened, suddenly Ronald Reagan was for gun control. But now? People would die. And it wouldn't be the cops. Or the National Guard that the government would send in. But if it's a bunch of white people waving confederate flags. Suddenly it's, Good people on both sides, again.

Somebody did a good joke the other day. Something like, The Flat Earthers are against social distancing because they are afraid of being pushed over the edge. I wonder what the Anti-Vaxxers will do if we end up with a vaccine for this thing? I want science back. Come back, Science, I miss you.

But, science. The new normal. Storm the Bastille all you want. Getting your minimum wage job back ASAP will not make your minimum wage job come back. 7-Eleven will never be the same again. That microwave burrito you are craving, it doesn't exist anymore. No matter how many faces you wave that AK-47 in. Facts are facts. They just found a U-haul truck in Brooklyn with bodies stacked in the back. Not because they were trying to hide bodies, but because there was nowhere to store them. They had run out of refrigerators. This pandemic isn't serious, it is fantastic. A thing of dreams. Of nightmares. Millions of Americans will die if we pretend that it doesn't exist. And the racist liars who hate the poor and only care about money, are funding these rebellions.

And we should all be pissed. We need to get money out of politics. The only lobbying in DC should be me lobbying my dick into Moscow Mitch's throat, and lobbying my balls on his chin. Turning him into a squeeze toy. Eyes popping out, and everything.

But violent imagery is not the answer. Dew collecting on the petals of a sprouting flower, at dawn, in a meadow. A fawn smells a flower. A bumble-bee's wings, tickles its nose. The tiny sneeze. Scared and elated, the fawn bounces away. A cool breeze. Bird song. A tree creaks in the distance. Leaves dance, and water falls onto the forest's floor. Clacking on dry leaves. A baby bird loses its first feather. Snuggled under his mother's warm bosom. The feather floats into the sunlight peeking through the boughs. A tiny rainbow appears. Morning on Earth.

Bacon and waffles for breakfast. With apple. Warm butter, and syrup.

DAY FORTY-EIGHT

G left. Greg came over. I gave him some beans. He called them, Feces water soaked in virus. Or something to that effect. I had left them on the steps when he and Professor Curly went out for a stroll. It wasn't mean, just an observation. Hopefully he got home with them alright. He was on a bike. They were in a paper bag.

Bacon and waffles for breakfast. With apple. Warm butter, and syrup. Lunch was fried chicken with garlic sourdough. Rice and broccoli. Red drink. Cherried Coke.

Made some brownies with G. Which was nice. She is very sweet. I woke up at 3a worried about her. I mean, she was born in the fall of 2007. The economy tanked just a few months later. Twelve years later, it is double tanking. There is a maniac in the White House. Who wants nothing more than to make it worse. A virus floating around. Capable of killing millions of people. And here she is. Getting her first period during lock down. At her dad's apartment. Excited for the future, like a normal little girl. I just can't stand it. It breaks my heart.

But she is resilient. And if we change in the right way. At least if school is done via computers, we will put an end to school shootings. That's a positive. Less airplanes. That's a positive. A new economy, that isn't just growth at all costs. That's a positive. The end of Old Folks' Homes. The Nuclear Family.

Things are dark. They will only get darker.

Salad for dinner. With croutons. Forgot the smoked paprika in the dressing. And the tomatoes were not the best.

The beans turned out great. Don't believe what Greg or Professor Curly tells you. Perfect beans. Top notch. Hats off!

Speaking of resilience. Professor Curly dropped off some laundry at the laundry. I have never, ever, been okay with having someone else doing my laundry. Two reasons. Maybe three or four.

1. I think you should do your own laundry. These are the clothes you wear. The sheets you sleep on. The towels you dry yourself off with. They are connected to you. You should be connected to them.

2. 2. Only people who aren't really connected to the world have somebody else do their laundry.

3. People with money have other people do

their dirty work.

4. Even if you don't have time to do your own laundry, you should make time. Connecting with yourself for two hours a week is important.

5. Having somebody else do your laundry is an invasion of privacy. [Just so you know, if you are a woman, the guy doing your laundry is smelling your panties while he whacks off in the back room every time you drop it off.]

6. It is financially prudent to do your own laundry.

However. I really hate doing laundry. Laundromats are disgusting germ fests. The televisions give me migraines. People are assholes. Who the hell has quarters anymore? There are too many smells. The place is always crowded. I really don't like folding things. If you Cost/Benefit the experience, it is worth it to have some dude shoot a load with your panties wrapped around his head. Give the dude a Rocky Mountain Cruster one time. He will get the message.

So in this time of need. In this time of descent. This time of fracture. When businesses need all the business you can give them. I have had a change of heart. Maybe it costs a little bit more. Maybe I don't one hundred percent have a direct connection to my clothing. But it beats getting the virus. It beats throwing up on the side of the building because of the digital television. It beats spending two hours lugging shit back, and forth between my apartment, and laundromat. More than once that is. Plus, it helps the local economy!

So in conclusion, things change. And I am changing with them.

Unrelated, I have to clean the bathroom and the refrigerator tomorrow. Professor Curly said her elbow hurts from the hand job she gave me. Something about trying to pick up a 40 oz beer that has been glued to the floor. Too big. Too much work. Just not worth it.

But then I wake up in the middle of the night. A straw in her mouth, and a bottle of lube in her hand. Smiling.

Mixed messages.

DAY FORTY-NINE

Seven weeks. Feeling optimistic. By force. Awards night. Steak and martini. Cleaned the fridge. What a pain in the ass. Once a year. I have no problem with a clean fridge. It's complicated. There are a lot of ins and outs. Tomorrow, the bathroom.

Party across the street. Mixed feelings. It is pretty nice today. Early moon.

How was the pleasant weather like a handsome pig? Because it is nice snout.

How did I know Professor Curly had the virus? She fat shamed me, which exposed her anti-body.

Egg salad for lunch. I really don't like egg salad. It tricks me every time. I feel like PW Herman. Although, when I was peeling the eggs I came up with this hot number, and then tried it out later. With hilarious results:

So I was peeling the eggs, and I kept asking you questions, but you never responded. I looked up, and you weren't there. Turns out it was just the smell. I thought you were standing next to me.

I don't like hard-boiled eggs. I never have.

Deviled eggs. Yuck. Texture. Taste. Smell. It's the yolk. Soft-boiled eggs are okay. Lots of salt, and pepper. Toast.

Professor Curly is hitting the sauce. Tonight. Her play has been nominated for: Best Director, Best Actress, Best Sound Design, Best Play, maybe Best Lighting, I can't remember. I also can't remember the name of the award. But it is all taking place via the internet. She should win them all. Her play is phenomenal. Good luck!

She is a lightweight though. Things might get sloppy. I predict dancing, and buttered popcorn. Brownies. Water, and a late morning.

A note from Greg about the beans:

Those are the best beans I have every [sic] ate. Ede is loosing [sic] her mind over a legume. We are in a bit of a pickle. Not about sparing your precious feelings you twinkly twat! More about making our mouth holes feel nice. Soothing our precious mouth holes you heaving pork snout!

XO G

Fantastic Boners [Boners is Norse for Beans, pronounced Benners]:

   1 lb pinto beans
   2 lbs cow feet
   6 broccoli stems [4 inch length, 1 1/2 inch diameter]
   1 ham bone
   1 bulb garlic
   1 onion
   salt
   3 tbsp of bacon grease

large pot with lid
wooden spoon
water
colander
large bowl
medium bowl
tongs

In the large bowl. Place beans. Cover with water. Two inches higher than the beans. Add one granule of salt for every bean. Stir. Place on top of the refrigerator. Go to bed.

In the morning, around 10a, take the beans down from the top of the refrigerator. Place on top of the counter. Put colander in the sink. Dump the beans into the colander. Rinse with cold water. Dump back into the large bowl. Cover with water. Two inches higher than the beans. Place back on top of the refrigerator.

Put large pot on top of stove. Turn to medium-high heat. Fry cows feet. This will take time. Fry the cows feet three or four at a time. They will brown. They will also make their own oil. Sprinkle with salt. Turn over with tongs. Place in medium bowl when browned on both sides. Repeat with remaining cows feet.

When every cows feet is fried, return to the pot. Cover with water. Bring to a boil. Cover. Reduce heat to low. Bubbling when covered. Steaming when uncovered.

Cook for hours. Add onion and garlic. You could probably just throw them in whole, but I cut the garlic bulb in half first. The onion was leftover from other stuff, so it was already cut up. Keep cooking.

Around 10p turn off heat. Go to bed.

In the morning, around 10a turn the heat back up to high. Bring to a boil. Reduce to low. Add ham bone, and broccoli stems. Work up a stink. A stink big enough for Professor Curly to complain about. Stink up the apartment all day. In the evening, remove the ham bone, and what is left of the cows feet, and the broccoli stems. With tongs. Strain the broth through the colander into the medium bowl. Put back into the pot. Dump the contents of the colander into the medium bowl. Put the colander in the sink. Take the beans from the top of the refrigerator, and dump into the colander. Put beans into the pot. Add water. Two inches above the beans. Add the bacon grease.

Bring to a boil. Reduce heat to low. Cover. Cook until bedtime. Turn heat off. Hit the sack.

In the morning, around 10a, turn the heat on high. When boiling, reduce to low. Cook all day. Stink Professor Curly out all day. Around 5p fill up an empty queso jar with beans, cover, wrap in a plastic bag. Place on the stoop for Greg to take home. On his bike.

Leave the rest of the beans cooking until bedtime. Around 10p. Turn off heat. Go to bed. In the morning, around 10a, turn heat to high. When boiling, reduce heat to low. Let cook for a couple hours. Turn off heat.

Later in the afternoon, when the beans have cooled. Place in an empty spaghetti sauce jar. Put lid on. Put into freezer. For Ron.

Best Actress!

The rest of the awards went to the Patriarchy for making life so intolerable in America that we are forced to make terrifying art at all times. So we don't all collapse in terror.

Optimistically. Speaking.

DAY FIFTY

Stocks up. Projected deaths are 3,000 a day for the month of May. In America. You know, if this was a novel, I would have ended it eleven chapters ago.

Cleaned the bathroom. Which was nice. To have something physical to do for a couple of hours. Although, I can't stand the smell of chlorine. It reminds me of swimming in high school. Which then reminds me of freezing cold evenings in the winter, in Wyoming, when you would get out of practice, and it would be dark out, and you would walk to the car with Matt, and he would have a cold, and he would hand you a menthol cigarette, and you would say, Menthols? and he would say, Yeah, I got a cold, so I had to switch. And the combination of freezing cold air, chlorine, and menthol cigarettes filling your lungs after swimming 5,000 yards. It was enough to make you puke.

Bonin' schedule is off. Did a half-bone a couple days ago, and a bj today. Professor Curly has been distracted. I don't blame her. She has a lot going on these days. Whereas, I do not. She had at least three hour-long phone calls today. In fact she is on one as I write this. I talk to G for about five minutes every day. At noon. During her lunch. But that is about it. Old habits. But it is a long tradition of emotions for me. If I call someone, then I end up missing them. Brothers, mother, old friends. Then I just feel unsatisfied, and lonely. Questioning the decisions I have made in my life. Maybe I am an ostrich?

Out of sight, out of mind.

Maybe this new communication strategy is good. Part of the problem with cell phones is that anyone can call you at any time. Then you either answer or you don't. But if you don't they will just call you back. Keep calling. Keep calling. At a certain point, the inertia of calling them back becomes too much. Because you have to spend ten minutes lying to them about why you never answered your phone. It is exhausting. But with this new protocol. You set a time, and date. Then you have the call. Then that is that. Zero manipulation. Pure intentions. Good faith. And it also addresses the fact that people have lives, and maybe don't want to be on the phone all the time. The novelty has worn off.

I usually let my fingers do my talking for me. Right? Professor Curly.

Guess we will have to go to the grocery tomorrow. Need supplies. I am thinking I would like to make cheeseburgers. But cruelty. Not for the animals at the slaughterhouse, which is a different debate, but for the workers. I mean, I haven't seen it yet, but I am sure it is out there, if you eat a steak it will kill an immigrant. And not in the negative, but in the flag waving, heritage types. Eat a steak, kill a Mexican. But then when meemaw dies it's a Chinese Hoax.

We have bottomed out. It has been a long time coming. It is finally here.

I just saw a neighbor come home with Trader Joe's bags. Two months, maybe, since I have seen that sort of thing. It makes me sad. The guy must have taken an hour out of his day, at least, to go to that Trader Joe's. To carry those bags home on the subway. It is a reminder that people really just want to go back to the way things were before this crisis happened. Nothing is going to change. It is only going to get worse. Local businesses will be decimated. Only corporations will remain. Subsidized by the government. Comply or die.

You can either eat this steak, and an immigrant will die, OR, you don't eat this steak, and your family starves.

Dunkin' for breakfast. Taco Bell for lunch. Outback for dinner.

I joke about Amazon Bucks, and Jeff Bezos being the person to bring us Basic Income, but it is looking more and more like, if we don't change our habits right this second, we are doomed to this fate. McDonald's will pay for road upkeep. Walmart will pay for hospitals. Starbucks will build housing. Et cetera. Et al.

But it is not just the meat in your fridge! It is the beans too. The lettuce. The whatever computer I am typing on. I understand the hypocrisy, I just don't have the money to ignore it. 90% of Americans don't have the money to ignore it. 90% of the world doesn't have the money to ignore it. Maybe even 99% of the world.

Sorry, Charley, I don't mean to be negative, but there are really dark days ahead. People are going to starve to death. Americans are going to starve to death.

But that is the thing with cheap meat. It is good protein. Chicken Backs are cheap as hell. So too, Cow Feet. But who wants to spend hours, and hours, making a Chicken Back/Cow Feet soup? When they can go to McDonald's, fill in a pot hole, and get a #3 Super Sized? With an apple pie.

There is hope. There is still an election in November. People seem pissed enough to flip the Senate. The racist liars who hate the poor and only care about money, seem to be getting what's coming to them. Well, at least the ones that don't understand that this will not end well, no matter how many times you try to polish the turd. That the Orange Douche is a sociopath. Who has no problem killing millions of Americans for his own political aims. Not that he really has any, aside from being in power, and avoiding going to jail.

Six months to the day. Yesterday. We can end this bullshit.

DAY FIFTY-ONE

Cinco de Mayo. Stocks up. Cheeseburgers. Temporary solution to my conundrum. Frozen hamburgers. Packaged months ago. I assume. It's not like king crab from Alaska. Or a lobster from Maine. Passive despicable. Not active despicable. Dirty martini. French fries. Frozen peas in stock.

Installed a shelf in the kitchen. Now we can put plants by the window. A touch of class.

Mariana came by. To get a hard drive. On her bike. I opened the window. Screen included. To say hi. Two flies got in. I let them back out later in the day. Maybe I should have let them stay? I mean, it is a little like, The Spirit of St. Louis in here. Charles Lindbergh was a piece of shit, but that movie was pretty good. The fly was his only buddy. Remember? Jimmy Stewart.

I just wrote a poem while sitting on the toilet:
When I think of all the poems written
but never read
and here I am
both male and white

begging for your attention

In my defense, though. The poems I was reading while on the toilet, sucked. And the inspiration for the poem was the imprint. Which, one time I found a library of their books on a stoop in Brooklyn Heights. Free to anyone who wanted them. Destined next to the garbage, or recycling, I suppose.

Professor Curly is going to hate that I just broke that wall. But she can suck it. Sitting around all day, winning Guggenheims, and having Zoom chats with Blondie. Crying about the awards she didn't win. While I wait on her, hand and foot, all day long, and when the cleaning is done, the dinner is cleaned up, the baby is put to bed, I can finally get a second to myself, to write down my thoughts, nauseous from exhaustion.

Oh, how the tables have turned.

I guess I will clean the windows tomorrow. It has been a year. We need more window cleaner. And paper towels. I should have been smart today. Bought some at the grocery. I wasn't smart. I got weird things. Short-sighted things. Cheeseburger things. The irony of suggestion. Projection: ironic suggestion. Accuse a dude of using the ultimate power of the presidency to make sure he gets a Big Mac, and suddenly you want to eat a Big Mac. Times are dark.

And what do you do with fourteen slices of American cheese? I guess we are hitting the brakes on the guts for a while. Maybe this time the torpedo will dislodge that toothpick I swallowed when I was eight. That fucker has been holding on to the edge of my guts more desperately than Tom Cruise in the beginning of Mission: Impossible 2.

Am I right!?

I still think it is funny that our landlord hasn't checked in with us since this crisis began. Schrödinger's Chicken. As long as he doesn't check in with us, and we don't check in with him, everything is just fine. But the second either of us reaches out. Bam! Our rent drops, and he has to move back in. However, this arrangement is working out just fine. We are both guard dogs, and tenants. Then again. He has three cameras, that I know of, watching the building. Probably others that capture the more intimate transactions of the apartment. Available on the Dark Web. For a price. Naturally. Like Charley says, If that is something you want to watch, go ahead. As he takes a roll of toilet paper from his backpack, and walks out onto a bald plateau on Carter Mountain.

And he is right, If you want to watch that, go ahead.

DAY FIFTY-TWO

Stocks are down. Slightly. If stocks are up tomorrow, after what is to be predicted to be the worst jobs numbers in the history of histories, I am going to re-think my moral stance on investing in the stock market, and suggest that we, the American working public, take all of our money, and do a reverse coup on corporate America. We should buy up all the stocks. Go broke doing it. Because if that is the only way we won't take a financial hit by the truly unconscionable disparity caused by both a corrupt Government, and a corrupt private sector, I mean, I don't know what else to think.

I did a thought experiment last night, 3a, when I couldn't sleep because of worry from the future. What would One Billion dollars really look like? And it looks like this:

1 Billion = 1,000 Million = 10 Million $100 dollar bills. Which means; If you put a guy sitting

at a desk, in Manhattan, on some street corner, and had every single person alive in the entire New York Metropolitan Area, line up, and hand the guy at the desk a $100 dollar bill, that would be $1 Billion dollars.

And if it took one second per person to deliver the money, the whole process would take 115 days. If my math is right. Not that that number really means anything. Or that even a billion dollars means anything. But if 40 million Americans are collecting $1,000 dollars a week in UnEmployment, which is $40 billion dollars a week, that we are hemorrhaging. Money, that is meant just to shore up the economy, so America won't collapse on itself, to stay afloat for another week, I mean, I really don't know how the stock market is seeing this as a positive thing. If I was China, I would sell off all of American debt at half price, and cut my losses. Fuck politics. The US is a sinking fucking ship.

On the other hand. I made a pretty tasty carnitas today. Thirteen hours. It took to cook. But it was simple.

Carnitas Quarantino:

    4 lbs pork butt [bone in, skin on]
    cupcake pan
    1/2 baking pan

salt
pepper
spices [unknown]
large pot
cutting board
knife
4 tbsp of lard
2 cups orange juice
large bowl

Put pork but in large bowl. Cover with salt, pepper, spices [unknown], a rub Professor Curly got from one of her travels. Probably cumin. And cayenne. Garlic. Oregano? Rub around on all sides. Place cupcake pan in the middle of the 1/2 pan. Face up. Place pork butt in the middle of the cup cake pan. Turn oven to 200 degrees F. Place the pork butt into the oven. Set a timer for Ten hours later.

Meanwhile, 10 hours later, remove the pork but from the oven. Let rest for two hours. The resting is mostly so the pork butt can cool down. Cooled down enough to handle. With your hands.

Meanwhile, 2 hours later, dump pork butt onto the 1/2 pan, remove all meats, and skins from the bone. Place into large pot. Add lard, and orange juice. Cook on a low heat, like a simmer, for 2 hours, or until the meat is not trying to hold itself together anymore.

Meanwhile, 2 hours later, remove from pot, and place back onto 1/2 pan. Spread the meat out. Evenly. Take the skin, and cut up into small chunks. Put on top the evenly spread meats. Set the oven to

Broil. Put 1/2 pan in oven. Broil with the door open until the tips of the skin becomes crispy.

Serve with a relish of onion, jalapeño, apple, tomato, and lime. On a corn tortilla.

This recipe is vague. The important part is this: you can cook a 4 lb piece of pork butt for 10 hours at 200 degrees F. If the bone is still in, and the skin is still on. My guess is that it could have been cooked longer. Maybe next time.

Washed the windows. Lunch, carnitas. Dinner, carnitas. Man, they were dirty. Industrial Revolution, dirty. A funny thing I learned about Henry Ford, who is later than the revolution, but is a direct result of the revolution, he initially paid his workers really well. Treated them well. But then the second he started losing money, suddenly, not so much. And we pretend like what is happening now is unprecedented. This exact thing happened nearly exactly one hundred years ago. "Captains Of Industry" treated their workers well when things were going well, but then, at the first sign of trouble, they pull the carpet out from under everyone else aside from themselves. And spoiler alert, things sucked after that.

It took a global depression, and a World War, before things got better. And those things only got better for the people that directly benefited from the system. First, the "Captains Of Industry," then the white working class.

Dirty windows now. Then broken windows. Stop and Frisk. Robert Moses. Rudy Giuliani. Mike Bloomberg.

I mean, they are already trying to shove it down our throats that we need to pull ourselves up by our bootstraps again. How many times can we do that? I feel like a hobo wrestling with a pair of pants hanging from a clothesline in a silent movie. Ya know? I can't pull the pants down because the clothespins are too tight, so I try to get inside of them while they are hanging on the clothesline, but then I find myself struggling with the clothesline too. I am spinning around, making noise. Suddenly the owner of the pants comes screaming out the back door, shooting at me with his shotgun. And I am trying to untangle myself. And the dog comes out, and starts biting my butt. But I get loose somehow. And I run away. But the dog is still barking at me. And the man is shooting at me. Yelling, Get a job you bum!

I had a job! I had a million jobs! I have been a dishwasher, a waiter, a bartender, a rigger, a carpenter, a barista, an actor, a cook, a telemarketer, a ticketer, an elevator operator, a writer, a musician, a model, a stagehand, a hatter, a drug dealer, a student, a dry-waller, a driver, a painter, a lawn-scaper, a taco-dog, a log-dog, a granola handler.

And here we are again. Back to zero. Vapor in the bank, no tomorrow.

The funny thing about this situation, is that it is the first time in my life that I have felt secure. I don't have to go out. Money comes to me. I don't hate my job. I enjoy my time with Professor Curly.

I am not sleeping the best, but that is whatever. Things are grim. And I know that things will only get worse.

But, however, I also know that making this record, these will be remembered as the good times. The laughable memories that will keep us alive in the future. And I can't help that. I also can't help but notice that this will only be a memory.

There are cold times ahead.

Let us eat carnitas today, because tomorrow we will be eating ashes.

DAY FIFTY-THREE

Well it happened. Stocks way up. 33 million now collecting UnEmployment. The real number of unemployed, probably closer to 45 million. What can you do? It is not like there are now 75,000 people dead from a pandemic, with that number expected to quadruple by the end of summer. But things are looking rosy.

I am so confused! Is the world just filled with idiots? What am I missing? There will be a depression. There is no indication otherwise. The Orange Douche will make things worse. Is everyone just betting that the Nazis can hide all the gold before the Americans get to France?

I don't know. I will give it rest. But this is not over!

Went to the dentist to get a haircut. I am starting to think we need some sort of curtain in that bedroom of ours. My body is no longer built for this sort of exhibitionism. Professor Curly's, yes. Mine, not so much. And the parts that are, tend to be stuffed inside a variety of holes. UnDisplayed.

B-Team New England Steamer for dinner. From the first batch. Cheeseburgers with tater tots for lunch. Carnitas for afternoon snack.

The landlord got in touch. Through his agent. Asking about signing a new lease. We asked if we could possibly do a shorter lease, for now, because things are a little up in the air at the moment. The agent suggested a six month lease. Hopefully the landlord comes back with an offer to drop the rent a few hundred dollars, and we sign a year long lease. Professor Curly thinks that is a crazy thing to think will happen. I think it would be smart of him, but she is probably right. He will probably say yes to the six month lease, or just kick us to the curb. Either way. It would be a pain in the ass to move, but living in the city is about to get really hard. It might be time to carefully consider a move to Vermont.

I am thinking that a 50/50 cash to bank account money is the way to hedge the fallout. Either cash is going to be useless, soon. Or your bank account will be wiped out, soon. Or maybe neither. I hope neither. But as always, Iron your money!

G is coming over tomorrow. After school. She says she is okay with hamburgers for dinner. I think I should go to the grocery for some more frozen waffles. Maybe an avocado. I bet she would like the carnitas. They are pretty damn tasty. But the salsa/relish might be too spicy. I guess I could get some more iceberg lettuce.

Professor Curly's dad, and stepmom came over. Virtually. For a tour of the apartment. Her dad is going into heart surgery tomorrow, and wanted to see the place before he died. Which is a really dark joke he made, but pretty funny. Professor Curly vacuumed because of it. Which was very cute.

Supposedly the New York primary is back on. Andrew Yang sued. I am not holding my breath, but this is good news. New York is a blue state that seems to be run by Republicans. Because, money. Even though we have a supermajority. But there is talk about Yang running for mayor of New York City. I would vote for him. He seems to understand that poor people aren't poor on purpose, and they can use all the help that they can get. Even if it means that rich people like him pay more in taxes. The problem is that he has Bloomberg behind him. Which is not a good look at the moment. That fucker is a menace. His anti-Trump ads are top notch though.

How To Add A Shelf To A Window Sill:
Note* Most window sills have an overhang. At least 3/4". If your window sill does not, then these directions will not apply.
Materials:
shelf
tape measure
1/16" drill bit
1/8" drill bit
counter sink
3" screws
1 1/2" screws

bit that fits screws
pencil
piece of wood that is something like 3/4"x 1"x most of the shelf length.
Method:

1. Place shelf where you want the shelf to be. Have an external eye have a look-see. Mark the shelf all around on the wall, so you know where it will go in the end.
2. Drill three holes into the piece of wood with the 1/8" drill bit. 1" from either end, and one in the middle of the piece of wood. Approx.
3. Line the top of the wood to the bottom of the line that you drew. Hold in place. Use 1 1/2" screws to fasten.
4. Cram the shelf in. Put in place exactly where you want it.
5. Drill down into window sill with 1/16" bit. The bit should go through both the window sill and the shelf. Do three separate holes. Wabi-sabi style.
6. Counter-sink the holes.
7. Screw the 3" screws in the holes.
8. Enjoy[1] your new shelf[2]!

1. When I did this in my kitchen, I used this painting my friend Mike StClair gave me 20 years ago. I stained the back with Red Oak stain. His signature was written in pencil, so it really shined through. No offense Mike, but that painting on the other side is not very good, but your signature is fantastic! And 20 fucking years I have been hauling that painting around with me! And the knives you make now are wonderful.
2. Also, the reason I put this extra shelf in, was so I could have plants next to the window in the kitchen. Without hogging up all

You can have your own reason for doing things, but those are mine.

the space. There is good light in there.

DAY FIFTY-FOUR

G over. Double sequestered. In the kitchen. Professor Curly is doing a video chat with some theater in Seattle. This may take all my focus muscle. Kraftwerk. Until I get yelled at for being too loud.

Job numbers for April came in. 14.7% jobless. Worst since the Great Depression. Stocks way up.

Cheeseburgers, and fries for dinner. Started a sourdough starter. Hopes are not high. Professor Curly accidentally drank too much at dinner. I tried to get her to eat a gummy. Before her video chat. To spice things up. Nothing doing.

Might snow tonight. Nor'Easter. Raining now.

Professor Curly finished her copy edit on **Etiquette**. Next stop Miette. Then finishing touches. Then ready to print! Not sure when the release date should be, times are a little rough at the moment. But you know what they say, When the going gets tough, the tough publish books. Right? Feel like I read that somewhere, once.

Keep Calm and Double Dong.

Peanut butter, and jelly/honey sandwiches for lunch. With apple. Brownie. Grocery had flour again. Small bags. 2 lb. I bought two. My relationship with flour has changed. What good is a 2 lb bag of flour? Why not a 1 lb bag? 2 lbs is too small to do a bread, but way more than you would need for anything else. I am new to the game though. So sue me.

Had a dream last night where a squirrel was flashing a group of people. Me included. But for some reason she had a full denim outfit on. And flashed us by opening her denim vest. Everyone laughed at her. Said she wasn't really flashing. Someone yelled, You have to show your butt! Everyone laughed. The squirrel ran away, upset.

Maybe related? Before that part of the dream I dreamed I was working at the Office Bar and Lounge, and suddenly Alvin from **The Cosby Show** was washing dishes, and I said, What the hell? It's like season two in here!

Really not looking forward to a second Great Depression. Maybe I should get, We The People, tattooed on my forearm, and join a Death Cult. At least then I would have something to look forward to.

Do you think the Fuddrucker Rebellion sees the irony in organizing a protest rally against contact tracing via facebook?

Kraftwerk is such a great band. Forgot how much I listened to them when I was younger.

Never thought I would have nostalgia for such a band. Life has a way of giving you lemonade. Milk, milk, lemonade.

Around the corner, fudge is made.

I am making Jello. I must have done something wrong. It has been eight hours, and it still won't set. I should have made the pudding.

Maybe that is why I had the Alvin dream. Cosby, Jello, pudding, sexualized squirrel, Alvin and the Chipmunks. B ut the denim and the second season?

People keep comparing the lockdown to *Groundhog Day*. The movie. That is a false analogy. In that scenario you live the same day over and over, and can't die. That seems liberating to me. No matter what you do it doesn't add up to anything, so do whatever you want. It is just you, and your memories. I would say the movie that is more like what is happening is, *Office Space*. You do the same thing over and over, until you die. Combined with *12 Monkeys*.

Office Space now, *12 Monkeys*, later. Don't go outside, or you will die.

I used to have a Brad Pitt vibe, now it's more like Bruce Willis. Minus the witty quips.

I coulda been a contender!

Wrong actor, but if you think about it, Marlon Brando is a combo of Brad Pitt, and Bruce Willis. Or vice versa.

Like a snail crawling on the edge of a razor blade. Slug? Whatever the line was.

I have tried to read, **Heart Of Darkness**, three times. I can't do it. I like the idea. But the work doesn't speak to me. I don't like broccoli, I never have, and now that I am President I don't have to eat it.

And all the sons say, I am the decider. Do do doo doo. Do do doo doo.

I hope Florida rots off of main land America, and sinks into the ocean. Never to be seen again.

DAY FIFTY-FIVE

G ditched. Blueberry pancakes for breakfast. With bacon. Apple slices. Orange juice. Carnitas for lunch. With macaroni and cheese. Six rolls of toilet paper left. Julia came over. Brought biscotti. Professor Curly got drunk at dinner. Off 1/2 a Martin [Male Martini]. Same as a regular Martini, just with a wipe of lemon on the edge of the glass.

Snowed a little. Cold. Salad, and macaroni and cheese for dinner. Fresh bread with garlic, and butter. Had to abandon the sourdough. Don't have the right equipment. However, making a bread with whole wheat is a nice change. It gives me ideas.

Nino called G. Very cute. He keeps trying to catch a trout. Not a bunch of trout, just that one trout. He is like the guy from *The Plague* who can't get past the first line in the book that he is writing. But once he finally does, Hats off! He also is a doctor, and he also loves that book, so maybe I am making more of it than it is. But I do like the idea of just catching that one trout that changes everything.

It might be time to retire. The idea of going back to the way things were feels exhausting. Spending my days trying to catch a trout in the morning, working in the garden in the day, cooking foods in the evening, writing slow fiction in the night. Then a nice quiet sleep. Without anxiety. Worry. Silence.

Shake it off! Right, Jack? This desire for comfort.

I mean. I know how this ends. It is not pretty. We have done this before. Normal might not work for me anymore. The idea of getting on a train. Crowds of people. The airline just sent my mom an update on the itinerary for the plane ride me, and G are supposed to take out to Wyoming in June. It is utter nonsense. We would have to fly down to Florida first, then Denver, then into Wyoming. On the way out. And on the way back, they would have us flying to LA first, then Chicago, then New Jersey. The flight already is like flying to Europe. It takes twelve hours just to get to Wyoming, then a two hour car drive. Now it's like flying to Australia. I don't think so. Hopefully my mom can just cancel the flight. Or we can move the trip to August.

Or we can drive out sometime this summer. Even that would take three days. And they would probably throw us in jail for two weeks when we got there. Not because of the virus, but because we are liberal dip-shits, with n-word plates on our car.

My god we need to vote these fuckers out of office. Even if you live in the blue-ist state there is, you have to vote this November. Every single vote is important. Make sure every person you know is voting. Start now. Don't stop until this is over. If the Electoral College can beat out a Popular vote of three million, we need to make it ten million, twenty million. Those red states will still be red when the votes are counted, regardless of how the elections turnout. The system is rigged against us. We need to accept this. And if we do this. We will win. And when we win. We need to bring the hammer down.

The Orange Douche is a foil. The Republican party is evil. They are using him as a distraction so they can do all the disgusting racist agenda, lies, and financial corruption that they can before America goes up in flames.

America WILL be over if we re-elect this jackass.

February 5th. Remember?

Ruth Bader Ginsburg is 87. Remember?

Michael Flynn pleaded guilty, twice, to lying to the FBI. Remember?

Get yourself right. There are no rules anymore. Everything is politics. Even this virus is being politicized. Canada won't take us. Mexico won't take us. This is life now. America is a pariah. Third world. Exposed. And we deserve it. In the middle of a pandemic the Orange Douche is trying to take health care away from 20 million people.

I had a dream where I was looking out the window, and a rooster showed up. It was running on top of the snow. Then it fell under the snow when it hit a soft patch. I guess the snow was pretty crusty before that. I yelled out to Professor Curly. I said, Hey! There is a rooster running on the snow! A typical rooster! Come check it out!

The rooster was black, had a redhead, and orange feet.

Then it flew to the top of a fence. Made some noises. Then bounced away.

Professor Curly never came to the window to check it out.

The rooster crows at midnight. That was the note you would slip under the door of the other swimmers when somebody was about to spark up a dooby when you had an Away Meet. At the hotel.

Also, The dog barks at midnight. The system was pretty loose.

There was kind of a small amount of weed in Wyoming. And most of the swimmers were pretty nerdy, so the system broke down pretty easily. And nobody could stay up past 9p because we were so exhausted from practice. But still.

That was the system.

DAY FIFTY-SIX

Eight weeks. 80,000 deaths. They say if we would have locked down just four days earlier the number of deaths would be cut in half. They also say the number of deaths is probably twice as much as reported. So there is that.

Made a potato soup. First successful roux. Which gives me hope for future gravies. Either I am learning patience, or I finally have enough time on my hands to absolutely commit to something like a roux, or a gravy. I think I might have pushed it a little far today, though. Both with patience, and with rich foods. Pancakes for breakfast. BLT's for lunch, with homemade bread. Cream Potato Soup with warm bread, and butter for dinner. Professor Curly is logy. Also, I was a dick all day. So, even if my patience is growing, Professor Curly's patience is growing thin. Even as we both expand into the apartment. Like that joke about painting your apartment. Every new layer, slowly the walls are getting closer. I even noticed today that the two copies of ***My Emily***

Dickinson that Professor Curly has aren't exactly the same size. Even though they are the same exact book. Same publisher. Same release date. One of them has an extra two blank pages at the end. What is that about? Are they fucking with us? And why the fuck did I notice that?

Schrodinger's Economy. Capitalism is bunk. There is no supply and demand. Not in the way that we have been fooled into thinking.

I listened to this guy today try and blame immigration for the low minimum wage. His reasoning was this:

If the large corporations, like Purdue, and Smithfield didn't have to pay such shit wages in order to keep their prices down, then the Mexicans wouldn't come into the country to steal those jobs from hard working Americans.

Which, maybe it is true. But maybe, just maybe, they don't pay shit wages in the first place, so hard working Americans could do those jobs, and actually earn a living. Thereby making it harder for immigrants to come and steal those jobs.

Once again they try and blame the consumer for the problems of the corporation. I mean, they expect the guy at the grocery to have a PhD in Corporate Practices in order to make the smart choice on the pound of bacon they are buying. That onus is not on us. It never was.

That is what I mean about supply and demand is a lie.

We have choices as Americans. In this capitalism. But most of those choices are bullshit. Take chicken backs, for instance. Chicken backs are cheap, because nobody wants to eat chicken backs, the name is wrong. But people eat chicken backs all the time. Every time you eat a whole chicken, you eat chicken backs. But then somebody gets wise to that sort of thinking, and you have:

Pork, the other white meat.

Which was an advertising adventure. They accidentally bred all the redness out of corporate pork, which made people nervous, but then somebody decided to convince the American public that white pork was better for you than red pork, so now we think that red pork is bad for us. Even though it isn't. In fact it is the opposite.

Beef. It's what's for dinner.

Got milk?

It's all the same shit. We don't have more options as Americans, we just have different packaging options.

There is no such thing as supply and demand. It is an illusion. There is no difference between Marlboro cigarettes, and Camel cigarettes. A red Altima is no different than a beige Altima. The color is different, sure, but the car is the exact same. We are fools. And we buy into it.

But jobs. What this world is going to look like after this pandemic is over. The idea that we will just go back to work doing jobs that make us sick, and possibly kill us. How the onus is on us, the consumer, the employee?

I hope the airlines fail. I hope the meat industry fails. I hope we stop buying phones made in China that are brought back to America that get marked up 2,000%. I hope we stop buying clothes that are made by children in destitute countries. I hope minimum wage is raised to $20/hr. I hope we start focusing on infrastructure again. Solar power. Universal health care.

The way we have been looking at the Federal Government is completely backwards. The Queen Bee is not the Queen of the hive, the Queen Bee is the biggest slave of the hive. She exists for us. We don't exist for her.

It is the same with these large corporations. They would not exist without us.

There is no hope. Give up first. The solution will present itself.

Schrodinger's Economy. It is supply and demand until the second you start doing business. It is surprising how little we all need to survive. On a daily basis. A place to live. Some food. Clean water.

Take one of those three things away. You are likely to die. However, if you have an abundance of those three things, you are likely to thrive.

Think about Astronauts.

Think about Hot-Air balloons. [Did I do this

analogy already?] It takes a whole community to build a hot-air balloon, but only a few people can ride in it. I think I did, I think I did.

Nobody wants more than they deserve. Not normal people. They might try to get it, but they won't think that they deserve it. It takes a special asshole to want more than he deserves, and parlay that into a pie-eating contest on a lifeboat while the Titanic is sinking.

Astronauts, Hot-Air Balloons, The Titanic.

Pie-eating contests, and special assholes.

DAY FIFTY-SEVEN

Went to the deli. Storm hit when I was walking back. Most excitement I have had in weeks. So sensory deprived that it seemed like I might die. I stood on the porch when I got back. Under the awning. Touched my eye by accident, without washing my hands. Now I might actually die.

New stats about smoking. Five times less likely to get the virus, but twice as likely to die from it if you get it. What bizarre odds. Five in the hand, two in the bush. One for the stink, two for the pink.

Speaking of the Shocker. My brother Charley one time led a gang of rag-tag boobs called, The Washakie County Shockers. That was their hand sign, The Shocker. Which, if you don't know what it is, it is when you hold out your hand, and bend down the ring finger. The idea is the index, and the middle finger goes inside the vagina, and the pinky goes in the butthole. Charley's nickname was, Danger. Brandon was, Brock. Matt Earl was The Duke of Oils, well that was my nickname for him. I can't remember what his actual nickname was. Luke was an honorary member. His nickname was, Caution, because he was Charley's brother, but also the wimpiest member. I am not sure what their mission was. Aside from getting drunk, and wreaking havoc. Maybe trying to get laid? They drove everybody nuts for a few months, then disbanded. A little bit of Washakie County history.

Stocks middling. States reopening. Despite nothing having changed. Despite every single indication that doing so will just make things worse. And the media falling for the lies coming out of the White House that there is a possibility that things will be just fine. Hiding CDC guidelines from the public. The Vice Douche's assistant getting the virus, the Orange Douche's valet getting the virus, the Douche's Daughter's assistant getting the virus. The media is officially useless. We are living in North Korea.

Made a fantastic bread today. G's mom brought a sourdough starter over when she picked up G on Saturday. From San Francisco. Over 100 years old. Whatever that means. I over fed it. And it erupted. I was doing a regular bread thing that I wanted to learn. A smaller loaf. With just flour and yeast and salt and water. But I added some of the starter because it was boiling over. Making a mess. And the results? Fantastic.

I guess bagels are next. Then beer.

All we gotta do is split this one beer, Adam [***Young Einstein***].

Well. It was, All we gotta do is split this one beer atom. Then Young Einstein blows up his dad's brewing shed in Australia trying to put bubbles in beer, and accidentally discovers E=mc[squared]. Then he spends the rest of the movie trying to put the genie back in the bottle because his beer recipe will blow up the world. But then he saves the day by playing rock and roll guitar. Fantastic film.

A plastic bin showed up in the parking lot/front yard. It has wheels. A trundle bin. No lid. Neither me, nor Professor Curly knows where it came from. Now it has a cardboard box in it. Not sure what to do about it. Kind of would like to see how it plays out though.

Cheeseburger and fries for dinner. The last of the burgers. Think I need to do a freezer re-arrange. There are things that should have cycled-out by now that haven't. Things I may need to give up on. Horrible cupcakes, for one. And the awful butter cream I made for them with the wrong ingredients. That is the thing about having starved for so long, you hate to give things up. Things come in handy. In times of absolute need. But right now, if I was to think about it, I would take the few dollars I have, and actually plan for a destitute future. But then again, how do you plan for the future while living in a city? At what point does your moral obligation turn into self-preservation? Both Charley, and Scott have told me about their plans for both the Winter, and next year. The few things I can do involve having enough dry goods on hand in case the electricity goes out. But my oven runs on electricity. I should probably be stocking up on canned goods, and water. Gaining access to a car, and converting my monies into gold.

Or better yet, spending money on an all weather tent, and sleeping bags.

This can go two ways. Things will be fine. Which they won't. Or things will get bad, which they probably will.

How do you plan for probably will?

Friday they say, the state will open back up. The city, they say, will be closed until the end of May. We can't ditch, and go to Vermont until the end of the month anyway. So that is that. But what about G? Her mom won't let me take her with me. Cellular service sucks in Vermont. How much worry can a person handle? Not that I could really do much here. But the guilt if something went horribly askew would be devastating.

At the moment it is a question of comfort. I can sit and spin indefinitely. Focus and self-discipline, are two things I have in abundance. But Professor Curly. But G. But G's mom, and partner.

I am not the decider.

So. Here I sit. Broken-hearted.

You know the rest [You probably don't!].

Came to shit, but only farted.
Maybe I AM the decider!

DAY FIFTY-EIGHT

Exciting stocks. Started down. Then up. Then tanked right before closing.

General Tso's Chicken for dinner. Had to make a Hoisin sauce from scratch, which meant that I had to make molasses from scratch. Turned out great. Minute rice. Broccoli.

Did another bread. This time with just sourdough starter. No yeast [active dry]. Professor Curly creamed her jeans.

Realizing why I think it is important for stocks to tank. That is the only time when there is an urgency from both the corporate middle and the racist right to do something to try and stem the bleeding caused by this global pandemic. Not that we will suddenly have universal healthcare, a living wage, and affordable housing, but if the sociopathic assholes who run everything suddenly don't feel so impervious to this dangerous, and deadly disaster, maybe they won't behave like the cavalier cunts that they are.

Not holding my breath. But it helps. Come down to the gutter, you fuckers. I'll stab you.

Had a dream where I was in a convenience store in Wyoming. My friend Matt, who works for the oil industry, was buying a pair of Crocs that fit over the shoes he was already wearing. Not sure what horrible Australian footwear has to do with the American oil industry, but I am sure I will find out soon enough.

I also dreamed that I bummed a cigarette from a drug lord that was sitting in the passenger seat of a van. He had just shot a friend of mine. He was impressed that I bummed the cigarette. He liked my moxie.

Mimi sent some celery seed. In the mail. For an egg salad upgrade. I guess I will try it tomorrow. Need more eggs, and some mustard. I will go to the grocery tomorrow. Already have the Creamer Loaf to serve it on.

The plastic bin moved onto the sidewalk. Guess that mystery is solved. The super did it.

Cleaned out the freezer. There were about eight bags of bread butts. Hurt my feelings to throw them away. But things have changed. Bread-wise. It's just hard to say goodbye. How do you explain yourself to something that seemed so important just a couple months ago? That they aren't as important anymore? Even if it is only symbolic?

The world is changing. I am sorry. I guess I am changing with it. It's not you, it's me. Send nudes.

They say the barter system is coming back. Nudes might suddenly have monetary value again. Not all is lost.

France is opening schools back up. All students must wear masks. The Muslim community said, What the fuck, man? And for good reason. Irony may not be dead after all.

Speaking of hypocrisy, they have introduced the Tri-kini. A bikini with a matching face mask. That you can wear at the beach.

> Molasses:
> 1/4 cup brown sugar
> juice of one lemon
> 1/4 cup water
> small pot
> spatula
> Put sugar, water, and lemon juice in pot. Heat to simmer. Simmer until the thickness of syrup. Stirring often. Set aside to cool. The acid from the lemon prevents the sugar from crystallizing.

The days are getting long. Supposed to be 80F on Friday. Might be time to go onto the roof to catch some rays. The cemetery is the only thing nearby that even resembles a park. And that has been closed for months. There is a car in the front yard. The street is depressing. We don't have access to the back yard. A very inappropriate time to not be middle class. Maybe we could install hammocks in the living room? We have plenty of sand. Professor Curly keeps bringing it into the bed with her. Lord knows where she gets it from. Who am I to judge?

Beer levels have dropped again. 2002 levels. Two things; getting up at 10a, and no hangover for Fifty-eight days. Also, no shitty job to go to. Also, no pressure 4h writing sessions every night. Fucking, down-right civilized. Who knew?

Now I just need some fucking exercise.

Maybe tomorrow.

I can buy some chewing gum, get my jaw-line tight. Push-ups. Sit-ups. Rooftop tan. Maybe then Professor Curly would love me again. For my fantastic looks. And not just my hilarious jokes.

And my sledge-hammer, bell-ringing dong.

Send nudes?

DAY FIFTY-NINE

Stocks tanked. Leftover Homemade Chinese Food for lunch. And then I said:

"You know what I like about Chinese food? It's Lo mein-tenance." And then Professor Curly said:

"I really hate that joke." Then I said:

"Soy sue me." Then she said:

"Ugh, I hate that one even worse!"

Soup and salad for dinner. PeriPprosecco. Noon bonin'. With the windows shut. There were kids playing somewhere in the distance. I could hear them. When the window was open. Loud bonin' is pretty rude. Years ago, when G was probably seven or so, I was staying with her while her mom was in Europe somewhere. It was a nice day. Early summer. We were going to have dinner out back. In the garden. She was helping me set the table, when there was a loud bonin' suddenly somewhere in the courtyard. Before she could notice, I ushered her inside to go get something complicated that would take a while. Thinking that if they were still making noise when she got back I would take her back inside with some other flimsy excuse.

The neighbor also had small children. Who were playing in the backyard. He yelled:

"Knock it off! There's children back here!"

The loud bonin' didn't last much longer. Not that they stopped on our account. I think they just finished. But it was pretty rude. All they needed to do was shut the window.

I'm not saying that I haven't been indiscreet. In fact, quite the opposite. But if you are going to do a loud bonin', for whatever reason, just shut the window, if children are involved. If no children are involved, let 'er rip!

Fuck those prudes!

Somebody mowed their lawn this morning. It was a nice sound to wake up to. Reminded me of Luke.

The future is starting to feel insane. The landlord is supposedly mailing a new lease for us to sign. We have two more months rent-free because of our deposit situation. I understand that he doesn't want us living here without any document stating the legalities, but we are also in the middle of a pandemic. A week from today? A month from today? A year from today? NYC without culture? Starbucks, 7-Eleven, Duane Read? $2,000 dollars a month to look at traffic and rats? The next gentrification won't be from rich white families, it will be from rich white corporations. The Amazon campus expanding. Google. Uber. Status Cuomo is laying the groundwork for New York to become the next San Francisco. My first instinct about Andrew Yang running for mayor, was I would vote for him. But I think I was wrong. I was wrong when I thought Bloomberg wouldn't cave to special interest because he was a billionaire. Corruption is exponential. New York isn't left, left-leaning, leftist, it is run by Republicans that aren't stupid. Republicans that can kind of see past their tiny dicks. Republicans that know that you have to trick the poor into thinking things are just okay enough to not rise up and kill you with pitchforks.

I don't know if we should sign the lease. A year is nothing. But floundering with indifference is just as deleterious.

I guess it is a question of where to be poor for the next ten years.

Vermont is looking pretty tasty.

Brooklyn be damned.

DAY SIXTY

Three million more new UnEmployment claims. Stocks up. Why does it matter? Professor Curly asked. It is not tied to the economy. Why does it bother you? I said:

Put it this way, when the stocks go up, rich people get richer, when the stocks go down, rich people get poorer.

Carnitas and oatmeal cookies. Mimi's Classic Egg Salad for lunch. Celery seed. Coarse grained country-style mustard. Professor Curly said she loved it. I will eat some later. My schedule is off today. Forgot to switch from slippers to shoes. Until just a few minutes ago. Couldn't fall asleep last night. Ended up sleeping on the couch.

Made the mistake of watching **Back To The Future**. Not much of lark when treated as allegory. Racism. Misogyny. American exceptionalism. Re-invented history.

A couple good things though. When Marty does his guitar solo, and switches from 50's rock & roll to 80's Eddie Van Halen. Also, Crispin Glover is a fantastic actor. The Professor is top notch, also.

Biff is the Orange Douche. Bully. Rapist. Sociopath. Succubus. Alpha loser. Everything he touches turns to shit.

Here is the problem, though. Marty's parents have two different realities where Marty exists. In the first one, Marty's mom and dad fall in love at a dance. They get together. Have kids. Marty is one of them. The dad is a loser his whole life, which drives his mom to drink.

The second reality, Marty goes back in time. He kisses his mom. She finds it gross. She then gets attacked by Biff. Marty's dad punches Biff. Then Marty's dad and mom go to the dance. Fall in love. Have kids. Marty is one of them. The dad isn't a loser his whole life. He writes a book, and Marty gets a new truck.

But in both of those realities, Biff is a huge part of their life.

In the first one, Biff is just a bully that treats Marty's dad like shit. In the second reality, Biff tries to rape Marty's mom.

I mean, we learn that Marty's mom is a really horny teenager. Which kind of gets her into trouble. And Marty's dad is a peeping tom. Which gets Marty into trouble. But everyone involved in this weird triangle has a vested interest in what the outcome will be.

But Biff is just a big jerk that causes mayhem. A

menace. Why would they keep him around? Just to rub his nose in it?

Are Marty's dad and mom in some Sub/Dom relationship with Biff?

If Marty's dad is the Dom, then he gets a fancy truck, if Marty's dad is a Sub, his mom is a drunk?

They have the same house in both realities. Marty has the same girlfriend. Are we to believe that time-travel is so subtle that the moments leading up to your parents kissing for the first time is the difference between being successful or unsuccessful in your life?

And what about Marty's uncle being in prison his entire adult life, for unknown crimes, combined with the fact that Marty asks his parents for forgiveness for starting fires when he was eight? That is a giant red flag for antisocial behavior. They don't address it specifically, but my theory is that Marty started the carpet on fire because he was trying to set the family cat on fire, but the cat ran away when he dumped lighter fluid on it, and he was already holding a lit match.

Or maybe that is why Steven Spielberg uses the same score for all of his films. Those are the noises he heard in his head right before he lit the cat on fire, himself, but before the fire department showed up, and his parents got back from their dinner-date.

We may never know.

Tomorrow was supposed to be the end of this.

Things change. They are opening up part of the state. New York is kind of large. I looked at a map today. It made me exhausted. Fifteen minute walk to the subway. Wait. Hour train to Penn Station. Wait. Two hour train to Albany. Wait. Five hour van ride to Buffalo.

Money is bogus.

You know, if we all decided in the first place that we should live like I think we should live, we wouldn't be in this predicament.

Just sayin.

Get a bunch of dynamite. Dig a hole. Throw all the dynamite in the hole. Run a long fuse. Fill the hole back in. Stand on top of the filled hole. Light the fuse. Blow yourself up. Where you land is where you are.

I don't want to go back to work.

I don't want a job.

I don't care. I am not good at it. I don't like it. I don't want it. It hurts my feelings.

What's the quote, Jack?

I would rather feel broken than numb, because feeling something is better than feeling nothing at all.

Something like that.

DAY SIXTY-ONE

I think I'll hurl myself against a wall. Cause I'd rather feel bad then not feel anything at all.

That is the actual quote. Slightly more poetic. Stocks up. G over. Carnitas for dinner. Sauteed chard. 81F. Jack-ass brigade on the streets. Sidewalks. Not a good sign. Just wear a mask. Please. You do that one thing, the transfer rate reduces four-fold. We have all been stuck inside for two months now. Just a little bit longer.

But whatever. Science is dead. The republicans killed it.

Economy lesson:

Professor Curly has been buying things online. Shoes. Outfits. Trying them on when they arrive. Changing her mind. Sending them back. The economy in action.

Someone starts a shoe company. Makes a shoe. Sells the shoe. Needs a box. Somebody starts a box company. Sells a box to the shoe company. The shoe company mails the shoe. Somebody starts a mail company. The mail company mails the shoe.

The person who bought the shoe gets the shoe. Doesn't like the shoe. Returns the shoe. The mail company delivers the shoe to the shoe company. The shoe company has a shoe. Sells the shoe. Needs another box. The box company sells the shoe company a box. The shoe company mails the shoe. The mail company delivers the shoe.

Now, you would think that the system doesn't work. There is no product actually being sold. Possessed. But you are wrong. If you were right, restaurants wouldn't exist.

The thing itself, the product, is merely overhead. The cost of doing business. The business itself is the business.

As long as there are more shoes going out than coming back, a profit will be made.

Think about it. When you buy things online, you give the company you are buying something from your money. They then send you the thing you bought. What happens if they don't send you the thing you bought? You have to go to them to get your money back. Because they have your money. To spend however they want to. But what if when you go to get your money back, they just tell you that the item you bought was on backorder. What if back order just meant that they were waiting for somebody to return the item that you bought?

I mean, if you created enough delay in your business that there was enough time in between when somebody bought something and when you would have to deliver that thing, you could essentially start a business, sell out your entire inventory, and then declare bankruptcy without once making a single product.

Sound familiar?

This is how the stock market works. This is how money makes money. What the government deems, Too Big To Fail.

It's not a Ponzi Scheme, or a Pyramid Scheme. Those schemes involve actual things of value.

This is where $2.5 trillion dollars went when the Federal Reserve freaked out a couple months ago. Down the fucking drain.

And how guilty do you feel about taking UnEmployment during a global pandemic that will kill millions of Americans if you don't just sit there and twiddle your thumbs for a few weeks?

I'm not poor, I'm an artist.

I'm not poor, I took a vow of poverty.

I'm not poor, the Fed let me down.

I'm not poor, my dad forgot to sign the will before he died. Now my fucking sister and her loser boyfriend are living in Paris, and won't return my phone calls.

I'm not poor, I'm roop. I just avoid srorrim.

T-shirt ideas.

DAY SIXTY-TWO

G left. Headed to the beach. Be back tomorrow.

Professor Curly bonked. Got the virus, again. 6th time? Says she needs a bonk donk. Whatever that is. Gonna be a long night. Pray for her.

Planning the exodus. Very complicated. Cabin in Vermont. June. Need to figure out how to get there. Borrow a car? Rent a car? Build a hot air balloon? Walk to New Jersey. Figure it out from there? Plants? Mail? Any exit plan needs a re-entry plan. Two week quarantine on both ends.

Need something. Fresh air. Exercise. Borrow a bike? Rent a bike? Go where? I didn't like the beach before the pandemic, what makes me think I will like it now? You can't swim. I like swimming. The sand is the same. I don't care for sand. I like to watch the airplanes land. But there aren't any airplanes any more. I guess I could just go to the street corner at noon, and give myself a sunburn. Rub sand all over my body. Get dehydrated. Sit in traffic, exhausted, on the way back.

Am I the only one that thinks about a woman's

vagina when they ride by on the back of a motorcycle? Giant vibrators on wheels. I mean, when I switch the setting on the faucet in the kitchen sink to the spray mode, and I run it over my hand, I get a funny feeling down below. What must a motorcycle feel like? That is direct pressure. Vibrating. And the way you have to position your body while riding on the back? I'm not trying to be a perv, I just see it constantly, out front. That must be a large part of the appeal of riding on the back of a motorcycle, right? Are these women just cruising around town squirting out orgasm after orgasm? Should I reconsider my stance on motorcycle ownership? You know, for my curly red friend?

Buy a motorbike? Gives new meaning to the Stimulus Check.

Seriously, though. We are reaching a crossroads. I am perfectly fine riding this out until time ends. But people are getting nervous. But what can you do? Get on a train, and go to Coney Island? Herpes slathered boardwalk? Shoot the geek? I could go for walks again, but there is nothing but sidewalk for miles in all directions. I have done those walks. Multiple times. Ignore the virus? For what? I am not certain I am healthy enough to beat it. For what? To endanger more people that are actually putting their lives at risk to combat this pandemic? For what? Because I am a little stir-crazy, and summer is here?

The economy is tanked. I accept that. Fourth time in my lifetime. Housing boom in the 80's that led to my parents declaring bankruptcy. 9/11. 2008 housing crisis. Now this. What's the big wow? Put a Democrat in the White House, and things will get better. Put a Republican in the White House, things will get worse. Financially. We have plenty of proof of that.

I am in no rush to build shit up again. Another ten years of destitution? What else you got?

I received an electronic mail today from the most reliable source that I know, that stated, in no uncertain terms, that the antibody tests are both unreliable, and useless. False positives, and there is not enough evidence that having antibodies mean you are immune.

Meaning! The only thing we have to fight against this crisis is testing for the virus itself. Contact tracing. And wearing a mask whenever you are around people. Full stop.

All this other shit. This splitting hairs about what we should do, or not do. The dichotomies. Contradictions. Is specious reasoning. Unless we know where this thing is, and who has it, we are just as naked now, as we were three months ago.

Avoid people. If you can. If you can't, wear a mask. Wash your hands well. Stay vigilant. Get tested if you can. Engage with contact tracing.

If you are okay with Facebook, but have a

problem with contact tracing, you are an idiot of the highest degree. A fucking moron.

Don't know what else to say. We can't ostrich this virus. It's AIDS, if the stigma of AIDS was actually true. You CAN get this virus from coming into contact with someone who has it. You CAN give it to everyone you come into contact with if you have it. There is no vaccine. There won't be one for months if not years. Even if there is one. And if there is one, you won't have access to it for months, and months after that.

But who knows? Maybe I should buy that motorcycle. Throw ten rolls of toilet paper into a backpack. Put the backpack on Professor Curly. Hop onto the motorcycle. Professor Curly on the back. Arms around my waist. Blow town. And when the cops catch up with us on the George Washington bridge, Professor Curly can squirt some oil slicks onto the road to send the cops squealing, and screeching into the dividers. Flipping them the bird. As her cotton dress flaps in the breeze. No panties. Butt exposed. Riding off into the sunset.

Hollywood-style.

General Tso's Chicken for dinner. Fried rice. Steamed broccoli. I am digging this recipe. It is really complicated. But cooking. Not baking. And ginger.

General Tso's Chicken:

1 lb chicken breast cut into 1 inch chunks[1]
1 egg
1 cup flour
3 garlics
2 green onions
3/4 inch ginger
sesame seeds
red pepper flakes
Sauce:
1/4 cup chicken stock [water will work, I am sure, but stock is better]
2 tbsp white sugar
2 tbsp white vinegar [rice wine vinegar]
1 tbsp sesame oil [preferred, canola will work]
1 tbsp Housin sauce [half-molasses tbsp, half-peanut butter tbsp]
1 tsp corn starch
bowl
frying pan
frying pot with frying oil
fork or whisk
wooden spoon
paper towels
plate
tongs

Put oil in frying pot. Put on stove. Turn to medium heat. Beat egg. Mix with chicken chunks. When the oil is hot, dredge chicken chunks in flour. Fry. Four at a time. When golden and floating, place on paper towel on plate. Repeat until chicken chunks are all fried. Put sunglasses on them. Set aside to, "Cool".

Mix all the sauce ingredients in a bowl. Whisk, or fork. Set aside.

---

1. If you think of it, marinate the chicken in soy sauce for a few hours before hand. The chicken needs salt, but not too much.

Cut the dread locks off the bottom of the green onions. Cut into 2 inch chunks. Chop up the garlics. Slice the ginger into something that you would eat. Not too big. Not too small.

Place frying pan onto stove. Add a couple tbsp of oil. Turn heat to medium-high. Fry green onions, garlics, and ginger until fragrant. Add sauce. When bubbling, add chicken. Stir. With wooden spoon. Keep stirring. Add sesame seeds and red pepper flakes. Stir. Remove from heat. Let sit.

Serve with rice and steamed broccoli. Soy sauce and duck sauce. And beer.

DAY SIXTY-THREE

Nine weeks. May 17th. Sunday. 90,000 Americans dead from the Coronavirus.

G came back. I made bagels. Surprisingly easy. Salt. Everything. Plain. Tasty. Carnitas for dinner.

Did some more thinking about the motorcycle scenario. How to express the absurdity of it. Imagine some machine that was driven by one person, and another person rode on the back. Leaning back, hands behind their head, a Fleshlight hooked to their junk. It would be weird, right? It's not just gender politics, and the patriarchy that makes that so. I see what I see. It's not my fault it gives me thoughts, Professor Curly.

What was nice about the bagels was the dough. What I have been searching for. A lean dough. They call it. Lots of elbow grease. Ellenbogen Fett, the Germans call it. Lots of kneading. Lots of resistance. Lots of time, an almost mindless activity. Plus, instead of having a loaf of bread in the end, you have little units of bread. With tasty toppings. The only thing I did wrong was use

All Purpose Flour, instead of Bread Flour. [Sorry Ramona, I led you astray. I had no idea it would come to this.]

They say the longer you boil the bagels the chewier the bagels become. I wonder if that is how the first piece of chewing gum came into existence? Somebody forgot they were boiling bagels, got a phone call or something, and then, bam! a bagel you could chew all day! Maybe when they left the kitchen to take the phone call the bottle of mint that was resting on the spice rack fell into the pot of boiling water? I bet that is how it happened.

Constitution Day in Norway. Seventeenth May. The Fourth of July for Norway. With respect to America, that is. Very intense holiday. If you ever get the chance, go check it out. I have a feeling it is what Nazi Germany was like on November 9th every year. Nationalism at its finest. Un-ironic, Unfettered. Unapologetic. And very, very white. Parades and beers. Polse. Flags. Snus.

Nine new cases in Worland. They just, "ReOpened". If a butthole town of 5,000 people in Wyoming can't escape this crisis, I don't know how we are going to beat this thing. I mean, you really have to be trying to get it in a place like Worland. You can go days without interacting with another person. Weeks, even months, if you feel like it.

Whatever, let's get back to the laughs.

G had me cut a cucumber into slim slices, and soak in vinegar for an hour, then cook at 175F for three hours. Something she saw on TicTac. A healthy alternative to salt and vinegar chips. Turned out like you would suppose. Not quite right.

When I was a teenager, my dad got heavy into making jerky. He bought a dehydrator. Sometimes the jerky turned out phenomenal. Sometimes, not so much. These cucumbers fall into the latter category. Lots of spirit, but wrong choices were made. Like a drunk cheerleader at a kegger, senior year. The consequences will in fact become legacy. Not a good look.

"Don't shit under the couch cushion! No! No! Oh my god, No! Did that just really happen?! Holy shit! Did you just see that?!"

Okay, that is a little dramatic with respect to the cucumbers, and the jerky, but true story. You don't live that shit down. An entire stellar high-school career destroyed in one drunken night.

But I do have some advice, since you asked:

Don't EVER shit under the couch cushions during a party. People can see you, and they WILL remember it.

Lykkelig Syttende Mai!

DAY SIXTY-FOUR

Stocks way up. G left again. More bagels.

Simple Bagels:
  large mixing bowl
  2 baking pans
  cooling rack
  large pot for boiling water
  plastic wrap
  hand towel
  kitchen brush
  small bowl
  whisk or fork
  spatula
  large knife
  Dough:
  4 cups flour [I used all purpose, they say that bread flour is better, I don't know if that is true, I used all purpose]
  3 tsp dry active yeast
  2 tsp salt
  1 tbsp brown sugar
  a little bit of oil to coat dough and sides of bowl during the rising
  1 1/2 cups warm water
  In large mixing bowl, add flour, yeast, salt, sugar.

Mix with hands until all the sugar is clump-less. Slowly add water with one hand, mix into flour mixture with other hand. 1 1/2 cups of water is merely a suggestion. In New York in May where the humidity is high but the temperature is moderate, I have found myself using less than 1 1/2 cups. How much less, I couldn't tell you. I just know I didn't use all of the water I measured out. Which was 1 1/2 cups.

Mix until you have a sticky ball of dough. Sprinkle some flour on your counter and place dough on top. Remove the dough that will be stuck in between your fingers. Add to dough ball. Knead. Knead like the wind!

You will have to keep adding sprinkles of flour as you knead. What you are looking for, is a dough that is neither sticky, nor dry. Not sure exactly how to describe this. But you will need to knead the dough for at least thirty minutes. At first it will seem like you are adding lots of flour so the dough won't stick to your hands or the counter. At some point you will stop adding flour and just be kneading. But as you continue to knead, you will find wet spots. So you will need to add more flour.

Eventually a thing will happen where the dough becomes really stretchy. Like something has changed. Bakers call this the Puberty Shift. Once this happens, knead the dough for another ten minutes. The dough will be dense and resistant, like a teenager. I think that is why they call it the Puberty Shift.

At this point, leave the dough on the counter. Wash the mixing bowl. Dry out. Pour some oil in it. Rub the dough in the oil, and wipe down the inside walls of the bowl with the oiled dough. Cover with plastic wrap.

Place near something warm. I use a radiator. Let rise for one and one half hours.

Shaping and Boiling:

Meanwhile, one and one half hours later.

1/4 cup approx. of honey

Fill large pot with water. Add honey. Place on stove top. Turn to high. Set to boil.

Place mixing bowl on countertop. Remove plastic wrap. Punch down dough. It should be about two times the size of when you left it last. Roll around in your hands for a while. Stretching it. Playing with it. It should be a little oily from the oil. Roll into a ball. Cut in half.

Cut that half in half. Roll cut halves into balls. Cut in half. Do the same to the other half. In the end you should have 8 equally sized balls of dough.

Take each ball of dough in turn. Roll in your hands until you have a perfect sphere. Find the exact center of the sphere. The north pole with your index finger. The south pole with your thumb. Pinch them together until a hole appears. Shove your index finger through the hole. Put your other index finger in the hole also. But in the opposite direction. Make a motion like you are trying to get somebody to speed up their story. Expanding the hole as you do this. When the hole is about 1 1/2 inches wide, shape into a good looking, "O". Place onto baking pan. Repeat until all 8 balls of dough are good looking "O"s.

Cover with towel. Wait for water/honey to come to a boil.

While waiting, place the cooling rack on top of the other baking pan. Next to the stove.

When the water/honey is boiling, place 2 bagels at a time in the pot. Boil for one minute. Flip over with spatula. Boil for one minute more. Remove from water/honey, and place on cooling rack.

Repeat for all 8 bagels. As they cool, but before they are cooled, rotate each bagel 90 degrees, that way they will have a cross on the bottom instead of just lines. I doubt this is important, but it is good for looks.

Leave to cool and dry. Drying is more important than cooling. Although, they are related to each other.

Flavoring and Baking:
one egg
spices
Set oven to 425F. Preheat. Mix egg with 1 tbsp of water. In bowl. Set aside.

I like everything bagels. Professor Curly likes salt bagels. G likes plain bagels. Whatever your preference is, brush egg wash on top and bottom of bagel. Add topping, nothing if plain, and put back onto cooling rack. When they are all topped transfer to the other baking pan. Still on top of cooling rack. I tried cooking them directly on the baking pan, but for whatever reason they bottoms cooked more than the top, which was fine with one batch, but this other batch was nearly burned. The third batch, I just cooked on the cooling rack. Problem solved.

Place in oven, Cook for twenty-five minutes. Remove from oven. Let cool.
Bagel bumpin' good times!

Addendum:
Everything bagels are tricky. The garlic likes to

burn. The onions like to burn. I think the trick is this:

> Place equal amounts of sesame seed, poppy seed, and kosher salt in a large bowl. Bigger than the bagel. Mix together.
> Mince 1/4 of a white onion, and 2 garlics.
> Slather bagel[s] with egg wash. Dip the top into the seed/salt mixture, making sure to coat the sides. Place on rack. Sprinkle onion and garlic on top.

I tried both dried garlic and dried onion. Neither could stand the heat, so they had to get out of the kitchen.

Also, the next time I make bagels, I am not going to use an egg wash with the everything bagels. I think I will just coat all sides with seeds and salt when they are still kind of wet, and just add some garlic and onion to the top.

The egg wash seemed to have its own agenda.

Works well for the plain bagels, and the salt bagels, though.

Speaking of tanning agents for bagel-faced douche-bags, the Orange Douche is now taking his own science concoction to ward off the dreaded Chinese Hoax. We are all going to die. It's every man for himself. The only glimmer of hope is that his Suicide Death Cult will actually drink the Kool-Aid. But their poor children.

Tom sent me this quote from Leonard Cohen the other day:

"Oh, and another thing, you aren't going to like what comes after America."

No, no we won't. And he is dead now. He was my Canadian sponsor. I will never get that green card. Canada was supposed to be the release valve! Mexico too! Now America is a powder keg lit from both ends. The only option is to explode.

I still get annoyed when I think of my friend Iver coming back from Norway, calling Americans idiots for electing the Orange Douche. First of all, you aren't Norwegian, you knocked a Norwegian girl up and moved over there, and secondly, fuck you! you are from Daytona Beach, fucking Florida! If anyone is the problem, it's you mother fuckers.

This is it. This is how it happens. This is what chaos looks like.

A gag order on all scientists working for the federal government. Firing any Inspector General that doesn't have political fealty. A maniac telling us to drink bleach, swallow a flashlight, and wash it down with aquarium cleaner. For prevention.

I don't know. I know I am supposed to just ignore this shit. Things are situation normal. But I disagree. You have to respect how stupid the average American is. How honorable ignorance is.

Not only do we get to experience a pandemic that will kill hundreds of thousands of us, Americans, for no reason, what so ever, we get to go through another Great Depression because of it, totally unnecessary, and! the richest among us will just get richer as this all unfolds.

Just go back to work. We all got to die sometime. What, are you a coward? God didn't put us on this world to be safe.

Yeah, maybe. But in the good times I was pissed off that we structure society this way. Now I am just supposed to ignore it because people aren't literally dying at my doorstep?

I got a job, I got a job killing all those cockroaches in that building of yours.

Bukowski was a dick. A racist, and his feeling about women was complicated, at best. But he did have one good point:

Nobody suffers like the poor.

And until we can all understand that, we can never move forward as a society.

DAY SIXTY-FIVE

Stocks down. Two rolls of toilet paper left. Three electronic mails away from hitting 5,000 unread. Not counting spam. Walked to the bank. Took out $600 dollars. Iron your money. The taco trucks are open again. Saw a dog called Tuna. Bought some cigarettes on Stanhope Street. Where Professor Curly used to live. Stanhope Street, not the cigarette shop. $10 dollar bargain. Her building had a ticket on the door. Trash violation? Murphey's birthday. Think she is going camping.

Bagels for lunch. Tacos for dinner. With broccoli. Sauteed. Tree branch out front that I should cut down. Maybe tomorrow. Going to poke somebody in the eye if I don't. Also, have an air conditioner that I need to take down to the street. See if somebody wants. Nice. Works. Too big for the window, though.

First real feeling of optimism in weeks. Mostly political. Older people are signalling that they are not buying the Orange Douche's bullshit. Fed Chairman Powell signalling that he is willing to do the right thing about how to deal with the economy. Biden signalling he is moving to the left. The Speaker of the House called the President a fat piece of lard. Which, as somebody who is constantly fat-shamed, I take offense to, but still. I'll take it where I can get it.

Need to go to the grocery tomorrow. Think I will make more bagels. Freeze them. Not sure what to do, though. Professor Curly loves them. Me, personally, I get my bagels from a can. But I do enjoy making them. And from what I have garnered, I lacked the sense to be intimidated by the process. The same thing happened with my rigging skills. It is nice to be good at something. And I have some ideas. But, also, like rigging, it seems bagels are dangerous. If Professor Curly looked at my junk, the way she looked at fresh bagels. I mean, I would finally have something to talk about with Willem Defoe. You know. Because she is a size queen. And he has a large one. And all the possibilities conjured in her mind. Toasted. Slathered in butter. Slathered in cream cheese. Hot out of the oven. Salted. Drenched in olive oil. Poppy seeds. Freshly ground pepper.

I hear that.

You know what they say:

Teach a man to make bagels, he'll fatten you up during quarantine, teach a man to have a big dick, you'll have a Bonk-Donk for life.

But 5,000 unread electronic mails. I

remembered when I hit 1,000. Six years ago? I want to say six years ago. I sent out a mass electronic mail. To everybody in my contacts. I was quite proud. And it is not 5,000 mails I just decided to not read, it is 5,000 useless mails that I have received that I didn't read. Haven't read. Blasts. Mailing lists. Group chains. I get an electronic mail about every week from SoundCloud. Which I have never, not once been able to open with any success. But they, for whatever reason, keep telling me that my account is about to be closed. I used to respond. Saying, Do it mother fuckers. Leave me the fuck alone. They never do it. They are lying. LinkedIn is another one. I remember Tom saying it was funny that he saw me on that website, six years ago. It is funny. I logged on once, because I was trying to find some information on somebody I had just met. Social media is a trap. Get off Facebook, now!

I don't know. Maybe we have reached the epitome of content fatigue? Sitting around all day. Fingers up our asses. I don't bother with the Washington Post any more. I find it suspicious that they are under-reporting the deaths from Covid-19. They are also really pushing sensationalism at the moment. Same with the New York Times. I use them as a check to whatever the Daily Mail is writing. Whatever transfers from the Mail to the Times deserves a second look. The AP is bunk, but it reflects what the Drudge Report is doing. Politico is actually a right wing media source. The Wall Street Journal has nice graphs about the stock market. The LA Times is just sports, and Hollywood. Facebook is idiotic. Get off Facebook, now! Axios is just ads for Walmart. Mother Jones lost me when I realized all their "News" was opinions. The Daily Beast gets it right every now and again. Same with Buzzfeed. But the only two sources that are worth shit right now, are:

What the Fuck Just Happened Today?, and the Onion.

Cross reference those two, and I think you might get a pretty good idea of what is happening in America.

But as I write this, I must confess, I was going to just leave things where the quote about teaching a man to have a big dick ended. But then I remembered that I left that nugget about the 5,000 electronic mails in the first paragraph.

Which was a dangler.

You can't leave a dangler, dangling. Even in times of great duress. Even in times of content overload.

You have to let people know how you feel when you say goodbye. You may never see them again.

Quit Facebook.

DAY SIXTY-SIX

Stocks up. Day of emotions. Walked to the bank. Took out $600 dollars. Iron your money. Counted every person I encountered on the walk. Unavoidable. 86. Some in masks. Some without. Really wish testing was ubiquitous. Starting to feel like Bad Boy Bubby up in here.

Ate twelve tacos yesterday. I bragged about it when I went to bed last night. Professor Curly was not impressed.

Been selling books in Norway, apparently. Heading to the Post Office tomorrow to send more over.

Did almost nothing I meant to do today. Slept like a donkey. Had some dream where I was giving this guy a haircut. When I went to cut the back of his hair, it turned out he hadn't had that part of his hair cut since he was a child. I was using an electric razor. When I got through the ancient hair, his neck was a tree trunk. Then, because of cutting his hair he suddenly was attacked by old memories. And the memories were very awful.

His mom and two of his sisters had been murdered by his father. Only he and his brother survived. The brother, because he was able to run away. The guy survived because his dad knocked him out with a baseball bat, so he was left for dead. The dad then blew his own brains out with a shotgun. It was a little bit of a nightmare. Slept on the couch afterwards. Kind of. Sleep isn't really the word for it.

Chicken pot pie for dinner. From the freezer. Still got two left.

Changed my pants. Tight and clean. Back before Professor Curly, and I had our first date, I created an intrigue by telling her I was wearing my best pants. She cancelled the date. But then, for some reason, she changed her mind. Then I got into her best pants. So the tables got turned.

The avocado seed still hasn't sprouted. Not sure when to give up on it. It's been more than two weeks. I got nothing but time, but still. It would be nice to see some progress.

There is a moment around 3p every day where I lay on the bed, on top of the covers, a shirt under my shoes, the window open. I listen to the wind blowing through the trees outside. The sound of the subway in the distance. Outside noises. Birds. Reading, **The Plague**. I last for about four pages before I drift into a liminal sleep. I come back around feeling refreshed. I have read the book a couple of times before, so I am in no rush to ingest it. But it is nice to have something of a cultural reference to this madness that is life right now. That people are idiots at all times, and for forever.

I miss science, though. I hope it makes a comeback.

I am almost 50/50 cash/bank. If things truly tank, they will both be useless. But at least I did something about it, right? My biggest fear is that the government will come hunting for money they think I don't deserve, because I fall below the poverty line, and therefore don't deserve any help, so they will just wipe out my bank account. Which, if there is any science left in the world, is the stupidest thing they could possibly do, but I wouldn't put it past them. And they would have to physically come get the cash I have. Which, I wouldn't put that past them either. But my theory is that they will have to stop printing money at some point, in order to avoid runaway inflation, so the paper money, maybe, just maybe, might be worth more than bank money. But all of this is just paranoia. If I was really that worried about it, I would go buy some gold somewhere. Or buy six shares of Amazon stock. I would be a millionaire by the end of the year.

But I would rather eat dirt until I die from malnutrition than contribute to the collapse of society. But that's just me.

Remember when banks would give you a small percentage of interest for using your money to make them richer? It wasn't that long ago. 1993? Now if you don't have enough money in your account to make them enough money they charge you money? They charge you money, because they don't make enough money from the money you lend them. You understand the "Service" they are giving you, is them taking your money and investing it in ventures that make them more money? AND! need I remind you that those ventures are considered so important that they can't fail? That if they start to fail, the government, our government, gives them money, OUR money, OUR tax dollars, so they can stay in business. And the business they are in, is making money from using our money to make money!

Drop out! Move out! Pull out! Quit!

No more houses! No more cars! Don't go to college! Don't get credit cards! Squat! Take the land back! Grow a fucking garden! Don't eat out! Get the fuck off Facebook! Stop buying shit from Amazon! Don't pay taxes! Eat only beans! Raise a goat! Kill the goat! Render the fat! Get another goat!

The world is officially unjust. And here we sit, dragging our cunts through the dirt. It doesn't need to be this way. All we have to do is say no.

It is either that, or the more simple option:

Sustainable energy through infrastructure. A living wage. Healthcare for everybody. Affordable housing.

The second option lets you keep your stupid stock market and your repulsive billionaires.

The first option means we cut your fucking head off with a chop-saw.

DAY SIXTY-SEVEN

Stocks down. 2.4 million new UnEmployment claims. Used the sourdough starter to make bagels. Fantastic. Slightly more dense. You have to bake for an extra ten minutes. Steak for dinner. Mashed potatoes. Green bean squeakers. Professor Curly is anemic.

Didn't make it to the Post Office. Tomorrow. Or take the air conditioner down. Tomorrow. Or cut the branch down out front. Tomorrow. Did manage to go to the grocery. Empty. Nice. No poppy seeds though. Seriously impressed with the bagels. Might think about starting a business. No money in it, but would give me something to do with my time.

$10 dollars to make 16 bagels. Sell them at $2 dollars a bagel = $32-$10 = $22

$925 dollars is my half of the rent. 30 days in the month. $925/30 = $30.83

If every 3 days I made a double batch. That would even out. I mean, it's not insane. I could work from home. I would probably need to get a license. And there is other overhead I would really need to consider if I was serious. But, I mean, it's not insane.

Lazy Kegels Bagels = Lagels Bagels

Lagels Bagels, The Loosest Hole In Town. Bagel-Wise. TM

Lagels Bagels, If Your Hot Dog Gets Stuck, We Return Your Buck. Bagel-Wise TM

I am starting to like this idea. Not the phony name, and the sexual nature of it. But the idea of starting a bare-minimum business that I can run out of my kitchen. Everything I need I can just get at the local grocery. This last batch proves that I can use All Purpose Flour, instead of Bread Flour. Three hours of work each day. Most of that, just waiting around for dough to rise, and bagels to cook. They would be "Artisanal" and I could market myself as an "Eccentric" so I wouldn't have to bother getting up at 4a to make them. They get there, when they get there. Mid-afternoon. After my 3p nap. I could still write at night. It's a win-win-win.

See! Like I been telling you this whole time, Capitalism works! Out of the ashes:

PC Bagels [Professor Curly's Bagels][Plus the reference to our tender times].

Murphey, if you are listening, can you draw me up a mock-up of what a PC Bagels logo would look like? I can make a shirt.

I mean, the original idea was to have a hot dog

cart. But the logistics of that seem impossible. Buy a cart. Own a cart. Store a cart. All things that would suck in NYC. Plus, hot dogs are kind of expensive. I can't make them myself. Buns are more expensive than hot dogs. Mustard? Onion sauce? Sauerkraut? Ketchup? I mean, need I say more? And! Heating the pans, washing my hands, having to stand on the street all day, serving hot dogs to jerks? What if I have to use the bathroom? I don't own a car, how do I get my cart around? Yuck.

I don't know. I think the idea is a winner. All I need is gumption. If I have love in my heart, and believe in myself, anything is possible.

So, I was joking that Capitalism works. Capitalism DOES NOT work. The Free Market works. You should be able to start whatever idea of a business you want. That is different than Capitalism. Capitalism just means one guy at the top gets all the money, and everybody else involved in making his ideas come to fruition can go fuck themselves and die in the process. Because there is no future. Nothing but money matters. The person with All the money wins.

A rat just ran up the steps as I was sitting outside. Which explains the mysterious bone that has been on the steps for some time. It didn't even bother being timid until I yelled at it. Then it ran away. What the hell? A cockroach did the same thing a few nights ago when I was sitting in the kitchen, minding my own business. Are the vermin getting desperate? They opened up Yellowstone park again, and the first thing I read about it is that some tourist got attacked by a bison. Not that bison are vermin, but I wonder. Mother Nature is just waiting for us to die. And for good reason. The other thing I read about Yellowstone was some idiot snuck into the park, and fell into Old Faithful, and burned herself pretty good. Human-kind is a fucking menace.

Last roll of toilet paper. I am calling it. Nine weeks and four days. 20 rolls of toilet paper. 68 days. Tomorrow, or the next day. 3.4 days per roll of TP. I guess I should have counted my own wipes, then I could cross reference Professor Curly's wipes. 1,000 sheets per roll. 294 sheets per day, roughly. Each sheet is 4 inches. That's 98 feet of toilet paper each and every day. That is the same amount of distance that if you sat at the End Zone on an American Football Field, and dragged your naked ass all the way to the 33rd yard line. Every single day.

Just sayin'.

I mean, I can account for about 1 yard of that toilet paper. Personally. Where does the other 32 yards go?

Just an observation.

DAY SIXTY-EIGHT

TGIF. Stocks rebounded last minute. G came back. Her half-birthday today. Cheeseburgers and fries for dinner. Already got three bagel orders. For next week. One for Sunday. And sent G's mom home with a sample pack. First you give them a taste. Then they come running back for more. Mimi thinks I should have a basket and lower the bagels down from the apartment on a rope. Like in Italy.

PC Bagels didn't catch on. Glory Hole Bagels? Phoenix Bagels? Sequestered Bagels? Budweiser Bagels? Bernard Brother Bagels? Bumpin' Bagels?

Didn't manage to get to the Post Office, or cut the tree branch down, or take the air conditioner to the street. I did, however, manage to acquire another air conditioner. You know what they say, When god opens a window, he crams an air conditioner in it.

Supposed to rain all day tomorrow. Hope so. Makes things easier. Chilled. Summer is coming pretty fast. Maybe not the best time to start a hot oven business in a small kitchen in a small apartment in a sweltering city. But who knows. Might be good to get a good detox.

Thirteen days. I am calling it. June 5th. Me and Professor Curly. Shades on. Cruising up to Vermont for a few weeks. Probably have to quarantine, but so what. Catch some fresh air. Take some hikes. Maybe even fish a fish. Then what, I don't know. Supposedly work is going to start again in July. Whether or not I can go upstate to Buffalo and back every week is a large unknown. Maybe instead of staying in a hotel we can convince the company to get a month long house rental. So I could stay there, and Professor Curly could come too. Mo and Eric. Scott and Grit and Miette. Jack if he still is into it.

Life. Am I right?

But that gives me thirteen days to perfect the bagels. Make notes. Adjust spices. Apparently my everything bagels are too salty. Although, that is criticism from the first batch. And that was a long time ago. A lot has changed since then.

Baking times are also an issue. The plain ones get darker on the bottom. Which is an easy fix. But just something to be aware of. I also need to have a secret ingredient. Which, at the moment, I don't. Ignorance, maybe? Hubris? A lack of confidence? Indifference? Too much free time? All of these won't last though. I need an actual, physical, secret ingredient.

I think I have a pretty good idea, now. Try it out tomorrow.

```
            1
          1   1
        1   2   1
      1   3   3   1
    1   4       4   1
```

FIBONACCI BAGELS

The "6" is both the Hole AND the Secret Ingredient. The other numbers are Flour/Yeast/Salt/Sugar. But the numbers rounded over. Like a bagel. Looking. Murphey?

Okay, that might be overthinking it a little. But that is better than, 4,3,2,1 Bagels, right?

Okay, relax. I am starting to remind myself of my friend Mike, who, when he started his taco restaurant, became obsessed with making hot sauces. They were all very tasty, but that is beside the point. Things take time. And no matter how many people you have taste-test your hot-sauces, you will never be satisfied. That is just not something you should force. Like maybe you should print out some fliers and go hand them out on campus? Or, I don't know, find a fucking assistant manager, instead of guilt-tripping your friends and family into working for free while you mad-scientist hot sauces all day and watch old movies at night because you are also writing a screenplay?

I don't know. I am a little starved for release

at the moment. A little mania never hurt no one, right? It's for the greater good. Like when a guy gets really muscley in prison. Except with bagels.

It's either this, or obsess about how the richest people in the world add hundreds of billions of dollars to their wealth as the world is literally imploding. I guess I can probably do both. We are going to need to eat something as we wait around to starve to death. Might as well be tasty. And have a good name.

I mean, here in a few minutes, G and Professor Curly will come out of their respective rooms, and we will all have a dance party. Things will get better. G's half birthday! 13 in November. 13! It's probably good she has been exposed to my poverty her whole life. Otherwise, she would be in for a pretty good shock here soon.

You can learn a lot from a dummy.

See what I did there? I compared myself to those dummy's in the car-crash commercials where they remind you to wear a seat belt if you are in a car. But I transposed it to being a dummy with respect to the economy crashing? Because I am poor, and am used to the abuse? And you can learn a lot from somebody that lives in the gutter when you find yourself in the gutter for the first time?

Pretty clever.

DAY SIXTY-NINE

G stayed another night. Pasta for dinner. With bacon, broccoli, and peas. Garlic toast. G's mom's bread.

The garlic I am drying turned green. I guess there is copper in the aluminum foil. Not sure what to do. They say it is safe to eat. Will address it in the morning. It was more that I was drying the onion, but I thought, Well shit, why not just add salt and garlic? Rookie mistake.

Think my business plan is already failing. There is a sense of dread looming. Never thought it would make money, but all the things that go into the business aspect of it. I am already exhausted. Although, G did come up with a really good logo:

tina bagel logo 3.jpg

The two finalist names are:

Tina Bagel [with no "S's"]

or

Lazy J Bagels

Lazy J is a branding thing. Like a "J" on its side. So it encapsulates both my rustic Wyoming rustler background, and my name, as well as my laziness about the bagels.

Rain all day. Didn't cut the branch down out front. G's mom said she would take the other air conditioner. Passed the responsibility of getting books to Norway off to the Publisher. Mailed in the applications for absentee voting. Hopefully the ballots get here before we take off. The primary is now June 23rd.

Was planning on doing a day sixty-nine love bonin' 69 style, but G is over, and Aunt Flo is in town.

Very last roll of toilet paper dangling in the bathroom. Went to the grocery yesterday. Professor Curly had one job. To get another 20-pack of toilet paper. She bought paper towels on accident. Now we have a year's worth of paper towels, but no more toilet paper. Tomorrow.

Nothing else to report. Professor Curly ordered a kitchen timer. She tried to order a glass scrubber, for drinking glasses, et al., but they are on backorder. I was going to shave today, but G took the bathroom mirror so she could do some clown make-up thing, for the internet. Somebody downloaded her design for a restaurant called Bread. I thought I had a hair on my back. I don't know how, but I convinced Professor Curly to take a gander. There was no hair. Then I somehow tricked her into giving me a back rub because of it. It was short, and I was standing up, but still.

I thought she might kick me in the shin. I swear it was there though. My dad had lots of hairs on his back. He didn't have very many hairs on his legs though. Because he wore jeans every day of his life. However, he walked around, "After Hours" wearing nothing but tighty-whities. Farmer tan from his fingers to where his t-shirt started. And from the neck up. Everything else was white as snow. Hairy up above. Bald down below.

Dad [A Poem]:
In after hours,
fresh out the bath,
Dad went,
the tighty-whities path.
A farmer's tan from his fingers parted,
up until his t-shirt started.
His neck and face,
the color leather'd,
hair on his back,
could not be tether'd.
Everything else,
White as snow,
Hairy above,
Bald below.

DAY SEVENTY

Ten weeks. 100,000 Americans dead from the virus. The Orange Douche celebrated by going golfing. G left again. Leftovers for dinner.

Afternoon bed bonin'. Been a while. Pretty quick returns. Two lick clit. Two pump chump.

They say that 20% of people left NYC. White people. Mostly rich, but also the youngsters who can't afford rent, who weren't born here. Good riddance. Don't come back. I give it three months before rent prices return to 2004 levels. Which is great. That is the kind of chaos worth looking forward to. Although, I suppose Status Cuomo will figure out how to subsidize Big Rental with subway monies, and sales tax, while maintaining the absurd market value rent hikes that exist now. But whatever, this is one of those instances where supply/demand is actually true. It doesn't take a genius to figure out that if you can get the same apartment for half the price in Clinton Hill, it is worth losing the $2,000 dollar security deposit.

But who knows, there is no shortage of snakes in the world.

The racist liars who only care about money are really trying to push this narrative that you are more likely to get the virus at home than you are to get it at work. Which is a hilariously specious argument. I mean, I guess the virus just miraculously shows up at home? Or that is where it starts? Should you just stay at work all day? Sleep in the subway? We are all doomed if that sort of logic prevails.

However, yet again, all that does is expose the already existing health structure we live with as Americans. No job security. No sick days. No health care. We constantly get each other sick for no reason. The only difference is that this time it might kill you. And your mom. And your aunt. And your grandma. Or, if the racist liars who only care about money would have you believe, your mom, your aunt, and your grandma are the ones getting you sick. Somehow.

Somebody yesterday was trying to make the argument that Republicans only care about the rights that the government is taking away, while the Democrats only care about the rights that the government gives you. And that was equal. And valid. That is not equal. That is not valid.

And I am not even going to bother to make an argument. Because it is useless. But I will say that if 100,000 Americans died, and the President was a Democrat, he would be in jail right now. Not golfing, not telling us to drink bleach, not firing every person that has oversight of his administration, in jail. In handcuffs, in an orange jumpsuit, on the porch of the White House.

The Constitution is a Government. Created by the people, and for the people. To protect ourselves, from ourselves. From corruption, and greed, and malfeasance.

For that aspect of our human dignity to be exploited for political gain in the middle of a global crisis, is disgusting.

We have to remember this. We need to remember this. We crossed the Rubicon on January 17th, 2017. The Orange Douche, and the Racist Liars Who Only Care About Money, did an end run, and came back to the river, and took a shit on the shores on February 5th, 2020. If we let this go on, they will do it again, and this time they will anal fuck our babies, and put them on pikes as a warning for anyone trying to defy them.

An end to America.

Nobody cares about your guns or your freedom of speech. Those things are intact. Forever. But forever doesn't mean anything if there are four more years of this insanity.

There won't be four more years. There won't even be one. The second the Orange Douche gets re-elected, life as you know it will be over.

You will not like what comes after America.

They say the measure of a man is how many bagels he can handle on his broom-stick.

Oh! I got a new one!

The reason I don't like oatmeal is because I find it gruel-ing.

DAY SEVENTY-ONE

America is stupid. A friend of mine tried to buy a car, but couldn't. Because they were on UnEmployment. The bank wouldn't let them. What does the bank care about how you spend your money? Not only that, but it seems like right now, of all times, having a car would increase your odds of being able to both find work, and do work. Especially if you live in the City. I mean, is the bank admitting that buying a car is a bad investment? Is it the bank, or the government? And if it is the government, how is buying a car any different than letting a corporation buy back its own stock with a bailout? I mean, you could argue that buying a car actually helps the economy, buying back stock does nothing for nobody except make the corporation more money, which they use to buy more stocks, and therefore have more money to buy stocks.

We do the cocaine, to have the energy to do the work, that will give us the money to buy the cocaine, so we can have the energy to do the work, that will give us the money to buy the cocaine.

Cheeseburgers for dinner. Tater tots. Frozen peas. Cold water.

Jess came over. Took a half order of everything bagels. I lowered them down on a rope. In a bag. We need a basket still.

Figured out a way to reduce my workload by 800%. Party bagel. I was kneading some dough today, and I wasn't paying attention. Accidentally created a giant bagel. Why not, right? I have never seen a party bagel. Party sub, yes. Party pizza, yes. Bagels at a party, yes. Just never a party bagel. You could do a transition topping thing. Start plain, end everything. Very stupid, yet genius!

Professor Curly got more toilet paper. 12 rolls. This morning I said:

Better hit the store today, babe. You're one turd away from wiping your ass with a throw-rug.

Thinking about buying a car. Trying to imagine what life will look like in a few weeks. A few months. The subway. Trains in general. Airplanes. Although the idea of owning a car in the city fills me with annoyance. Hurts my morals. But I don't see any way around it. Can afford it at the moment. How long before it becomes an albatross? Dangling around our necks? I don't even have a driver's license. Can you imagine dealing with the DMV at the moment? In NYC? And gas? Insurance? Tags? Inspections? Parking tickets? Parking? Professor Curly has a different disposition. She might actually use it. She likes the beach. The open parking lots, I mean, road. The specious notion that being able to drive to Albany, NY is somehow a good American freedom. It makes me hot, bored, and slightly car-sick, just thinking about it. But then again, I once walked ten miles to collect $40 dollars from Ross Johnson because I was so broke. So don't listen to me about the nature of freedom.

Freedom is just another word for nothing left to lose.

I have nothing to lose, so I answer to no one.
Therefore:
Freedom means answering to no one. Except roads. Traffic. Gas companies. Tire companies. Mechanics. Insurance companies. Emissions testing. The Department of Motor Vehicles. Banks. Titles of ownership. Big Wiper Fluid. Big Transmission Fluid. Big Air. Big Cassette Deck Lobby. Big Map. Big Seat Bead. Big Smell Tree. Big Spare Tire. Big Jack. Big Radiator Fluid. Big Car Wash. Big Wind-shield. Speed limits. Bad gas from shit food. One thousand miles of horrible landscape between New York and Wyoming. Will Hunting driving like a maniac trying to get to California before Skyler ditches his loser ass for somebody with a future.

I mean, If you think about it. The last scene of **Good Will Hunting**, Will is driving on the open road. Heading to California to win Skyler back. His buddies had bought him a car for his 21st birthday. But there is no indication that he even knows how to drive a car. True, he is a math genius, and he has been living on his own for what seems like many years, but what does that have to do with his ability to drive a car? There is no montage in the movie where he learns to drive a car. They infer that he is the alpha-male in their friend structure because he gets, Shotgun, but it seems like that implies that he is like the, "True Cowboy", he doesn't have to drive, and he doesn't have to open fences.

All I am saying is, Will Hunting would be a menace on the road. He doesn't have a license. He most likely doesn't know how to drive a car. He has spent his entire life in South Boston. He would probably get distracted driving, and start writing equations on the wind-shield causing a massive pile-up just outside of Philadelphia.

I was thinking I might write the treatment for Good Will's Hunting Too.

When Will gets to California, Skyler is shacking up with the creepy Teacher's Assistant of her favorite professor. Instead of just meeting Skyler and telling her he is sorry and he loves her, Will enrolls in the college, and takes on a secret identity. Enrolling in the classes of the Teacher's Assistant that she is dating. Things get more and more complicated as he gets closer, and closer to

Skyler's inner circle. At one point he has to pretend to be Asian, then a Pakistani woman, then an African prince. In yellow-face, and brown-face drag, and black-face. Finally everything blows up in his face at a fancy party the Dean of the school is hosting. Skyler finally recognizes him as a Mexican server, and they run off to Caltech, where Will invents a motorcycle that is so fast that he wins the Daytona 500.

I can change my identity, but I can't change my feelings underneath.

Just One Of The Guys meets ***Soul Man*** meets ***Breakfast At Tiffany's*** meets ***Bachelor Party*** meets ***Revenge of the Nerds*** meets ***Still Smokin'***.

Like a Party Bagel, on weed.

DAY SEVENTY-TWO

Stocks up, cocks up. Just joking. Cocks at half-mast. Chubs.

Parker came by. Lowered down a half order of plains. Found a basket.

Professor Curly is drinking lots of water. No lunch. Cecina tacos for dinner. Two types of beans. Tortilla chips.

City is starting to feel crowded again. Not a good sign. Thinking about buying a car. A gateway purchase. A house will follow. Then a job. Then the cool silence of death.

Feel like I should divulge my secret ingredient for the bagels. Just in case things don't work out. The secret ingredient is:

Tasty Flavor

The new plan is to buy a car in New Hampshire. Rent a car down here. Drive the rental to New Hampshire. Own a car. Drive to Vermont. Hang out in a cabin for a few weeks. Drive back to Brooklyn. Spend the next ten years moving the car from one side of the street to the other side of the street. Sometimes go to the beach. Freedom.

Hot 97 blaring across the street. Very aggressive. But, the DJ just said:

"60 minutes commercial free! But 6 feet apart! We ain't playin' around. Masks, scarves. C'mon guys! Bein' safe!"

First feeling of solidarity since this thing started. My god. How easy it is to bring people together. Division is on purpose. Grab em' by the ballot box. Vote! Vote like the wind!

For some, shyness might be their Covid-19! For others, a lack of education might be their Covid-19! For us, Covid-19 is a big scary virus who wants to kill us. And as sure as my name is, [Name] the people of [Name] can conquer their own personal Covid-19, which happens to be the actual Covid-19!

It's-a-sweater!

Three Amigos! was a good movie. I went to Steve Martin's apartment once. He has a large fondness for Picasso. He also seems really depressed. Nice apartment, though. Overlooking Central Park. West Side.

Have you ever taken a look at Central Park from an apartment on the West Side?

Have you ever taken a look at Central Park from an apartment on the West Side, on weed?

Just joking. G was about eleven months old. She crapped her pants during Steve's big speech to the rag-tag group of downtown theater friends he invited up for some sort of celebration. She cried the whole time when me and her mom changed her in the bathroom. Interrupting his speech.

He pretended he didn't care. He was lying. He was very upset.

Such is success.

Shit your pants during the speeches you are at, not the speeches you wish to attend.

DAY SEVENTY-THREE

Stocks finished up. But it was quite the ride. Mechanical Bull Market.

Dinner of chef's choice salad. I chose a Chef Salad. Secret ingredient? Anchovy paste in the dressing! Courtesy of Parker.

Washed my hair. Conditioner. Shaved. Went to the grocery. Thought about going to the bank. To get more cash. Iron your money. But it was too hot. And the idea of dealing with 86 jerks didn't really appeal to me. Tomorrow. I guess.

More proof that contact tracing fears of government overreach is unfounded. The previous tenant received a birthday card from his grandparents. I typed his name into the internet. The first person that showed up. His social media came up. I looked at some old photos. Recognized the apartment in one of the pictures. Sent him a message. I mean, how is it overreach when we willingly just advertise? You can't rape the willing.

But then they tear-gassed a group of protesters today in Minnesota. Who were protesting the death, by cops, of an unarmed black man. Show up at the State House with an AR-15 and demand that Fuddruckers is reopened, that is just freedom of speech. Show up at a protest and demand police accountability, without guns, that is considered civil unrest. White privilege is toxic.

I just saw the MILF from the back yard, out in the front, on the sidewalk! She nearly poked her eye out from the low hanging branch that I need to cut. Her kid was on a scooter. The DILF was wearing shorts and flat shoes. They had masks on. I didn't recognize them until they circled back around. Ugh. I should have paid more attention. We haven't seen the tattoo guy with his dog in a while. And all the trees in the back are full of leaves, so we can't really see shit anymore. I am starting to think that there will never be any scandals. The honeymoon is over. Lockdown-wise. Now it is just boredom, and low-grade nausea. At this point I think the DILF would have to croak, and then the affair would just be a bitter type of bonin'. Without scandal, or intrigue, or urgency. Just two empty souls trying to pass the time. And the guy with the dog and the tattoos, would just be an annoying lay. Selfish and conceited.

Turns out buying a car is complicated. Who knew? I have only owned one car in my life. An 1980 Oldsmobile Cutlass Supreme. For $200 dollars. From the daughter of a friend of my mom's. I took really good care of it. At one point, Kim, who had previously owned the car, saw me driving around town, and said to her mom, Christie, who was good friends with my mom, How come that car never ran that good when I owned it? Christie responded:

"Because he takes care of it."

I sold it back to Kim for $200 dollars. Lord knows what happened to it. Luke thinks we should get a Prius. The old ones are cheap now. With good warranties. I don't care. A car's a car. The whole point of a car is to take you from one place to another. And to eat gas and oil. Pollute the environment. Give money to Big Insurance, the government, and hucksters that call piss, lemonade. But what do I know? I am living like a statue as the rats take over the city. Hungry as hell. I think we will all collectively know that shit is truly fucked up when somebody films a rat attack a pigeon. Undeniable.

It is not that I am anti-car, or anti-"Freedom". I just don't get it. Choosing a car is like choosing bacon, it sure would be nice to afford buying acorn-raised, free-range, organic, conscientious bacon, but all we have to choose from is: Urban Meadow, Smithfield, Oscar-Mayer, and the repackaged bacon that somebody dropped on the floor in the cooler in the back. There is no real nuance. Visually, maybe. Maybe. You can choose the color. Or if you can play compact discs, or whatever. But, whatever.

Since I have been writing this, I have drank three beers. Budweiser, Narragansett, Becks. They are different. Kind of. But they are all doing the same thing. I mean, I prefer the Budweiser, but that doesn't mean anything. I won't not drink the other beers. That's all they had at the grocery. It was either, this, or that. It was either, these beers, or no beers. Can you pick up what I am laying down?

I would love to drive around in a Jaguar. How about instead of cars we have teleportation? We can eat a lobster roll for lunch in Nantucket, then go to Peter Luger's for dinner. Followed by drinks with Obama in Hawaii. And then do a line of coke on the ISS with Tom Fucking Cruise.

I am not against freedom. But freedom isn't a flavor of Kool-Aid.

Freedom is getting a bad haircut, then growing it back out.

Have you ever gotten a bad haircut?

Have you ever gotten a bad haircut, on weed?

DAY SEVENTY-FOUR

Stocks down. 2.1 million more Americans filed for UnEmployment. Seven days left. Hell or high water. Getting out of this shit hole. Maybe G can take care of my plant? I mean, I think the plant is almost exactly a year older than she is. It's like her older sister. I got it from a Home Depot as a little seedling when I moved in with G's mom.

Shiver got a leash. Not sure how you walk a cat, but the thought is pretty hilarious.

Carnitas.

Lazy J Bagels is closing shop. Too much work. Too much work to make. Too much work to digest. Tasty wild ride, though. Memories to last a life-time. RIP Lazy J Bagels. The secret ingredient was 1 cup of Budweiser.

4 cups of flour. 3 tsp of dry active yeast. 2 tsp of salt. 1 tbsp of brown sugar.

1,1,2,3,4 I guess Ramona was right, the Fibonacci numbers are, 1,1,2,3,5 what can you do? A good idea is a good idea, regardless of the facts.

Shame is a thing of the past. Math died long ago. It was us that killed it.

Jess came over. Brought some cranberry juice. Very nice.

Slightly related, because I did yell down from the window, as he and Professor Curly socially distant chatted on the front steps, "Hey Jess!" "Hi, Joey." "You on Facebook?" "Not at the moment. I deactivated my account." "Good!"

More and more evidence that social media tears us apart. It does not bring us together. As promised. And on purpose. That lie that you get in touch with people you lost touch with, that you wouldn't be in touch with otherwise. How it is good for business. How you are "Heard". The great equalizer. All bullshit. All just a money making scheme. For sociopathic billionaires who could care less how society works out. It is toxic. It needs to stop. You, you yourself are responsible for the outcome.

Normally I would disagree. Large corporations create an environment where as a consumer you don't really have the time or energy to realize you are making ill-informed decisions. The onus is on them. Like buying bacon. Or a car. $6 dollar bacon versus $20 dollar bacon. What do I care about bacon? I abstractly care about pigs, but that doesn't mean that $20 dollar bacon is better for pigs. It just means it is three times more expensive than the other bacon. I mean, I have one choice for groceries. What they have is what they have. I buy things that say organic on them. Especially eggs. But what about everything else? Flour? Coffee? Tortillas? I don't fucking know. I sit there staring at bacon choices. Trying to remember who is the biggest asshole. And I know that they all are the biggest assholes. Urban Meadows is probably Oscar Mayer, but with different packaging. Just $2 dollars cheaper. Realistically I am not going to stand there doing research on my phone to find out who is a lesser piece of shit. Not that my phone can do that sort of research, but that brings me to my point:

Quit Facebook. Do it. Do it right now. You don't need it. It makes the world a worse place. You are being morally hypocritical if you continue to use it. Quit Twitter too. For the same reason. For that matter stop using Amazon.

I mean, these companies don't exist without our compliance. You want the Orange Douche to stop fomenting hate and racism? Quit Twitter. What's he going to do? Call up the New York Times and say a bunch of racist things that they will then cover like it's news? I mean, they will, but not in the way that they cover it now. They will say, the President called us up and said a bunch of racist things, here is what he said. Instead of:

Good People On Both Sides, Trump Says

But whatever. I don't expect results. But I will

give you some context. There is an article that I read in the Onion many years ago that read:

Grandma Checks Her Email One More Time Before She Dies

The things that we all find important are disintegrating. Soon we will find the core to our beings. And if we are not careful, the sociopaths among us will inherit the earth.

Me, personally, I will be fine. Sociopaths like me for some reason. I see things that they don't see. Which they find useful. Beneficial. But whatever. This is a warning.

Take it.

The naked dancer is back. Something about her antics reminds me of that scene from, **Major League** where the female owner comes into the locker room after the game, and the team Manager, who is an old man says:

"We are out of towels. I am too old to go diving into lockers."

Read the room.

DAY SEVENTY-FIVE

Stocks middling. Protests. The Orange Douche blaming every port for the storm he created. Pure madness. The people burned a police house down in Minneapolis. I laughed when I read that. But I hate cops with a passion. Did I ever tell you I had to sue the police force in Worland when I was a teenager? For harassment. Cops suck. All cops. They are civil servants. They shouldn't have guns. They should walk around, or bike around, or ride around in those tiny little cars, and hand out tickets. That is all. All the other stuff. The violent stuff. I am sure we can figure out a way to deal with. If we try hard enough. And believe in ourselves.

Well it's official. I am the bad boy of cooking now. And not in the tattoos and cocaine way. I gave Greg wet brain with the beans I made. Now I have turned Professor Curly into a foie gras goose. I am sorry. Don't follow my recipes. Things will not end well.

Years ago, and on the other side of America, a

friend of mine really loved this scoundrel with a large dong. What he loved, however, was heroin, and sleeping with other people. Long story trunked. Herpes. I'm like that. But with food.

G was supposed to come over. But Professor Curly isn't feeling well. Pray for her. It's not the virus this time. I think you can only get it 4 times. Just joking. I don't think they know much more about the virus today than they did three months ago. Aside from that it spreads by airborne droplets, so you should wear a mask when you are around people. And wash your hands. Frequently. Avoid large crowds. Public transportation if you can. G might come over tomorrow. Depending. I was going to send her up to Mimi and Nino with more bagels, but now I am gun shy. Hubris is terminal.

Although. Corn Pops did show up in the apartment a few days ago. Right about the time bad feelings started.

Remember when Biden did that speech about Corn Pop giving him grief at the pool when he was lifeguard? Or that story he told about the kids playing with his white leg hairs? That was pretty funny.

I am all in for Biden, now. I will campaign for Biden when the time comes. He could rape somebody on 5th Avenue, and I wouldn't care. Okay, that last part was hyperbolic, but you get my point. I mean, if you want plug-nosed politics, you got them. I really can't think of what Biden could do at this point to lose my vote. Which is funny. It is the perfect antithesis to owning the Libs. The Orange Douche is just that disgusting. Just that bad at the job. Just that racist. Just that in the pocket of corporations. Anti-science. Anti-reality. Anti-American. I mean, we don't even need to have a Presidential candidate. Just a box cut-out of a human looking thing that says, Not Trump, on it. I would vote for that.

But, you know, the mail-in ballots came today. For the primaries. And the small amount of ink that Tom Perez was trying to erase from the ballot, is truly deplorable. The DNC should get their fucking shit together. And also, we should stop saying the word liberal, or Liberal, use Progressive. Liberal is meaningless. Also, forget about the word Centrist. It means nothing as well.

Progressive means; healthcare, job creation, personal liberty. Workers rights, and a better tomorrow. An end to racism, classism, discrimination. Small business, and the end to money in politics. Progressives are anti-lobby, anti-corporate monopoly. Pro-infrastructure, pro-American worker. Pro-science, and pro-fiscal responsibility.

But if you must use the word Centrist. If you must defend what the media, and the racist liars who only care about money call the Radical Left. Gently mention that all that that means, being to the left of center, is that people should have access to healthcare. All the other shit, gun rights, speech, states rights, all of that is covered in the constitution, and is not going anywhere. All we are talking about is how to protect the average American from debilitating debt, access to cheap medication, and a government that has the people's best interest in mind. Not the billionaires, and not the corporations, and not the lobbyists. The average American, who just wants to go to work, and feed their family, and hope for a better tomorrow where cops don't kneel on your neck and kill you because you write a bad check while being black, or give taxpayer monies to a company to develop a vaccine for a virus that is killing hundreds of thousands of Americans, only to turn around and sell it back to us at a huge profit.

Progressive means anti-corruption. Anti-brutality. Anti-kids in cages.

For some reason the Christmas tree smells now. It didn't smell before. Not in December, or January, or February, or March, or April, or most of May, but now, and for no discernible reason, here we go. Did it just give up the ghost? Silent but deadly? I mean, it does look dry, finally. But the needles aren't falling off. Fire hazard? It is next to an air conditioner now. I guess we should throw it out. But does that mean my avocado seed will eventually sprout? Is time relative?

I mean, the energy from the tree seems like it is

equal to how big it is, but also, like how much light it gets doubled against itself.

But that is crazy. Because if it is true, than that little Christmas tree we have sitting in the corner of the anteroom is like a fucking tinder box.

I mean, let's think about this. Mathematically. If the energy, or e, of the tree, was equal to the mass, or m, and the speed of light squared, or c2 then e would equal mc2, or e=mc2.

Then boom!

Bubbles in beer!

All we got to do is split this one beer, Adam.

DAY SEVENTY-SIX

G stopped by. I did 20 sit-ups. Spent most of the day in socks, long underwear. No shirt. Professor Curly had some business in the outside world. Longest time we have spent apart in seventy-six days. Five hours. It was ***Risky Business*** all over again. Except all I did that was risqué was go to the bathroom with the door open. Which was awesome.

Whitey's on the moon. 100,000+ dead from a virus that kills black people three times as often as whites, and whitey is on the moon. 40 million+ unemployed, and whitey is on the moon. Cops are murdering black men with almost no repercussion, and whitey is on the moon. Protests in 30 American cities, and whitey is on the moon.

Will somebody read the fucking room right now! Anybody?

Tacos Guggenheim for lunch. When Professor

Curly got back. You know, I made this salsa the other day. I used a cheese grater to grate everything. Onion, garlic, jalapeño, tomato, apple. It just didn't work. It was like there was too much flavor. No restrictions. Boundaries. But then last night I fried it for a while, and it became really tasty. But my worry though, is that there are some secret liminal thought processes that are unexpressed in cooking, that can't be defined. Like dark matter, but with flavor.

The reason I say "worry", as opposed to "thinking", is that I make this mistake every now and again, but for no real reason. I made the same salsa again, but instead of grating the ingredients I chopped them. The results were vastly different. The exact same ingredients. The exact same proportions.

Maybe our tongues are just stupid? Maybe we are living in a digital universe? Maybe there is a hierarchy of flavors? Like how Norway makes mediocre art. In general. But then they have people like Knut Hamsun. And all the rest of them are Jo Nesbø. Nazi sympathizers versus socialists. Would you sacrifice **Hunger** [Sult] if it meant that the only books you could read were by Jo Nesbø? But by doing so you gave every person in Norway access to health care and the liberty afforded by their version of socialism? Tough call. But then if you had socialism when *Hunger* [Sult] was written the book would have been a completely different book, and probably wouldn't exist.

And if suffering makes great art, does suffering also make great food? American food is shit. Norwegian food is shit. Their bread is fantastic. But in general, it is bland and mostly hot dogs and liver paste. But then their American fast food is phenomenal. Expensive as shit, but phenomenal. The Whoppers from Burger King, specifically. But that is because they don't use the capitalist model that we use. Their "Dollar" menu is priced accordingly.

I don't know where I am going with this. Just that my salsa failed. And I am confused as to why.

June 8th. It is official. New York re-opens. Whatever that means. Things are about to get even nastier. Warranted racial unrest combined with a pandemic. We just might see Marshal Law. Add that to the poorest among us starting to starve and become homeless. No leadership at the top. In fact the opposite. A race-baiting President. A huge portion of the population in complete denial of systematic racism. Add heat, and a predicted brutal hurricane season, caused by humans. Drop your socks and grab your cocks. As Scott would say. Bend over, and kiss your ass goodbye. The plane is crashing. The pilot is huffing gasoline, and the co-pilot is frantically racing through the plane manual wondering what all these blinking lights mean.

But whatever. It is situation normal. Just stop reading the news. Both sides. The Fuddrucker Rebellion must see the irony of protesting when just a week ago they were up in arms about how the Chinese Hoax was spreading like gangbusters when people in Florida went to the beach. Suddenly it's something else when you can just kill a black man for whatever reason you want and then hide behind the law? Hypocrites.

How is it different for a bunch of white supremacists to show up at the Capitol Building with assault rifles forcing the government to open Fuddruckers because they need to get their meat on, and the cops do nothing, call it a peaceful protest, but if a bunch of non-white people show up to protest, without guns, to beg the cops to stop murdering black men, you don't let them protest, you instead shoot them with rubber bullets and tear gas? Is it any wonder they burn the police house down?

I feel like somebody should start a Highlights magazine, "How are these pictures different?", but for White America, and Black America.

Just this fucking year, this year, 2020, instead of dealing with how the price of the subway was a tax on people of color, the MTA and the NYPD spent $2 million dollars hiring people to arrest people jumping the turnstiles. How are your profits now? You got a coral reef on wheels. And things will not change any time soon. I hope you find the grave you dug for yourself comfortable, because that is where you are spending your future, you racist bastards.

But whatever. You want phony race riots, or do you want actual race riots? Too late now. And it is not about distraction or false equivalencies, it's about human rights. American rights. Something people are actually willing to die for. And you may have the guns. But you do not have the numbers.

No one can save you from your ice cream sundae dinner now, man.

DAY SEVENTY-SEVEN

Eleven weeks. 106,000+ American deaths. G staying the night again. She has school tomorrow, so I get to see what modern schooling looks like.

My question is, what is the logic of sending in a large police presence to a protest against police violence? What result do you expect?

Drama Desk awards got cancelled. How are they the adult in the room?

Cheeseburgers with fries for dinner. Fried broccoli. Cold water. Professor Curly's dad's birthday. Turned 80. Was given a three-wheeled bicycle for a present. Hopped on it. Rode off towards T-Bonez Steakhouse. Never to be seen again.

Growing up, there was a guy who rode around town on a three-wheeled bicycle. Shaky Joe. He had Parkinson's. Pretty rude nickname by today's standards. Although Worland is still very tone deaf. He would probably get the same moniker today. And if you made the mistake of pointing out that it was an inconsiderate thing to call him you would be called a liberal dip-shit, say it was their free speech right to say whatever they wanted, call you a bleeding heart, mention that somebody they knew has Parkinson's, and then claim you are ruining their life.

"But," you could say, "it's not about me, or how I feel, it probably makes him feel bad when you call him that. How about instead of making him feel bad, you just don't call him that any more?"

"He's an adult. He can stand up for himself."

"But why does he need to stand up for himself? How about you just don't call him that?"

"Liberal dip-shit. How come you guys are always trying to take our speech away."

"I am not taking your speech away, I am just pointing out that you are hurting his feelings for no reason, and you should stop."

"Oh you Libs and your bleeding hearts. I live in the real world. It's not all just feelings."

"Well, I do live in the real world, and in the real world, you are being a dick."

"I'm being a dick? What about you? Coming here telling me what I can and can't say, taking my freedoms. For your information I have a good friend with the same shaky disease."

"Parkinson's. You have a friend with Parkinson's and they call it shaky disease?"

"You're putting words in my mouth! I said I have a friend with the same disease. Why are you guys always twisting our words?"

"But I thought I was keeping you from speaking. And what do you mean by, you guys?"

"See what I mean!"

"My only point is that if you weren't being a dick, none of this would be a problem."

"So you can just come in here, take my speech, ruin my life, and suddenly I am the asshole?"

"Okay, well, I guess, okay."

"Hard to argue facts, huh? Go back to faggotville fag-face!"

I don't know what my point is. Follow your heart. Do what you think is right.

My question is, why is my nose-bone trying to break out of my nostril? Why now? I got slugged in the nose about 15 years ago for no real reason aside from being in the wrong place at the wrong time. Is my nose trying to tell me something? Is it a metaphor? I can't quit touching it. It is starting to hurt. I mean, I can't put a bandage on it and let it heal. It's on the inside of my nose. The only real thing I could do would be to wear a nose plug for a couple of weeks. Is it a sympathy injury? Psychosomatic? I guess just wait and see. Stop touching it. Maybe it is just the weather.

Everything is just wait and see, now.

It is exhausting. Even for a guy who believes you should give up first because the solution will present itself to you. I want to go for a walk without thinking about it. I want to get drunk and pass out on the subway. I want hangovers and slow days filled with sleep and Chinese food. I want bondage and well-fed rats. School shootings. An airplane every thirty seconds. I want a root canal. Early mornings for a job I hate. Every minute I find myself sequestered from society I get stronger.

I can't get any stronger!
Give me crack and anal sex
Take the only tree that's left
And stuff it up the hole
In your culture
Give me back the Berlin wall
Give me Stalin and St. Paul
I've seen the future, brother
It is murder

I have two problems with Leonard Cohen. 1, he is the epitome of the patriarchy. 2, after he came back from his "spiritual cleansing" he found out that his manager had stolen all his money, so he went on a world tour to make his money back.

Should he have been a pauper for the rest of his life? Yes. Because, 1, he never would have been, he was Buddha at that point, he should have just traveled door to door spreading the word. And, 2, we need genius to be willing to be poor. Money is dirt. And there is no amount of arguing that will convince me otherwise. The more money I have, the less money somebody else doesn't have.

But whatever. Everyone likes money. So I know

I am not going to win any friends with this argument.

Follow your heart. Do what you think is right.

> "Go that way. Really fast. If something gets in your way, turn."
> *–Better Off Dead*

John Cusack got pepper sprayed in Chicago at a protest. And here, all this time, I thought he was an asshole. I mean, he probably still is, but at least he is doing the good work now.

Credit where credit is due.

See You Sack.

DAY SEVENTY-EIGHT

Protests in 100+ cities. NYC under curfew for first time since 1943. Orange Douche hiding in his bunker. Looting. Riots. Almost certain US military will get involved. Covid-19 cases sure to spike.

Stocks up.

Uno de Juno. G left again. Modern schooling was pretty funny. Got up early to make breakfast. By early I mean 830a. School started at 9a. G came out around 11a for a 5-minute break. Wanted a snack. Went back in until 1230p. Rest of school day got cancelled so the teachers could have a discussion about how to talk to the kids about the protests and the killing of George Floyd.

Pizza for lunch. Pepperoni and green olive. Hubris burned it a little. Was surprised that G ate it. Sent her home with fresh bagels. 2 plain, 2 lightly salted, 2 sesame. Also, some carnitas, an extra bag of corn tortillas that I am not fond of, but were good for her and her mom. A lime, and that funny salsa I made with the cheese grater.

DMV tomorrow. Which is right next to the Barclay Center. Hopefully will get some insight into whether or not it is safe to join the protests without it being a complete dereliction of moral fortitude with respect to the virus and my daughter and the ability for my daughter to see her grandparents.

I mean, we must protest, we must. If not now, when? Logically I can say, Well, New York City, for the most part has done a pretty good job of sheltering in place, personally, I have severed physical ties with nearly everyone I know, aside from my daughter, her mom, and Professor Curly. I will be wearing a mask. I doubt I have been exposed to the virus, or I have taken every precaution that would expose me to the virus. Meaning, I won't show up with the virus. G is going to Connecticut on Thursday. I won't see her again before that. In theory Professor Curly and I will rent a car on Friday and go to New Hampshire where we will pick up the car she bought. But then things get complicated again. Her mom is 78, her dad just turned 80. If we want to join the protests we won't be able to see her parents. And even if we don't see her parents, what does that mean when we get to Vermont? We would need to quarantine anyway, but what does it mean to everyone around us at that point? Professor Curly thinks we should get tested before we leave town, anyway. But what does that mean? Standing in line for three hours, and then the act of getting a test will most likely expose us to people with the virus, right?

I don't fucking know. I don't know, I don't know.

How the hell do you do a cost/benefit right now? I mean, the cost is obvious. Selfish behavior leads to illness at best, death at worst. Well, nothing at best, death at worst. On the other hand, do the protests need one more middle-aged white guy screaming into the wind? Probably not optics-wise, but spiritually, I would argue, yes. Pretty profound to see cops kneeling in solidarity with protesters. Bus drivers refusing to take arrested protesters to jail. Cold comfort, but at least there is some hope.

If hope is what we need right now.

I don't know. I guess we will walk to the DMV tomorrow. Four miles. See what happens. Temporary plates for the new car. I can pay my fine from ten years ago. Set in motion my getting my license back. See about the protests, and walk back home. A gigantic day out. I think I should pack us a lunch. With drinks, and snacks. Maybe Ramona will be around.

Weather should be mild. I should remember to remind Professor Curly to put on sunblock.

DAY SEVENTY-NINE

Stocks up.

First outing since the beginning. Eight miles of walking. DMV was closed. Too early for protests. Target was open. Bought some printer ink. Still unclear about how to get out of town on Friday. But a plan is forming. Will probably have to delay a couple days. Still. There is hope. Everyone seems exhausted. Same shit, different day.

Carnitas on bagels for lunch. With cilantro, onion, mayonnaise, cheddar. Salt and pepper.

Found some poppy seeds. Also, freeze-dried garlic. Black sesame seeds. Think I will try a new bagel recipe tomorrow. Not with respect to ingredients, but with respect to method. I think my boiling water is wrong. I am also having second thoughts about the egg-wash. I think that the water acts the same way as the egg-wash, but the egg-wash cooks too fast. I also may reduce the boiling time. The bagels today were too chewy. Oh, also, I think my secret ingredient is bunk. If anything I should use the opposite of beer. But what is the opposite of beer? A noose, and a belly full of glass?

Beer doesn't taste good, it just proves to your taste-buds that everything else tastes like shit.

I just think my recipe got too complicated. I need to pull it back a bit. I wish I had a bottle of that water that Charley brought down from the spring at the base of Carter Mountain. That was some damn good water. Cold and clean. Glacial.

Always had some idea I would write a political play called, **Theater Roosevelt**. The main character would be Gerald Fjord. Never got past the naming process though. Slick Willy. Dick Army. Maybe a musical. But those times have come and gone. Nobody wants to watch plays about straight white men singing songs about liberty anymore. For whatever reason. I mean, if I can't catch a break, what does that mean for America? I blame culture.

Culture dictates.

I mean, if the President of the United States can't tell the world that he is willing to send the United States Army into American cities to quell justified American protests, tear-gas peaceful American protesters outside of the White House so he can walk across the street and wave a bible in front of a burned-out church, what the fuck chance do I have?

Back when I was a teenager, some of my best thought experiments involved doing just that. I would be so rich, so powerful in the future, that everybody would have to do everything I said. All curfews would be abolished. I would have X-ray vision so I could see anyone's boobs I wanted. School would start at 9a, instead of 8a. Pizza every night. For dinner. I could choose a different bike every time I went for a ride. Homeroom would be the only class. All the bullies would have detention every day. Tanya would like me instead of Daniel. I could just use a special wipe that would remove all my acne. I would have my own room. That my brothers weren't allowed in. They would make movies about my thoughts. I would be handsome. And tall. And when I finally did the thing I was supposed to do, to change all of world history, they would give me a giant parade. And all the jerks I knew my entire life would have to sit there and watch me in the back of a limousine waving. While Mrs. Loschen showed me her boobs without my X-ray vision. Maybe try and secretly rub one out, if possible. If Luke and Jade were asleep.

Then I would fall asleep. And wake up in the morning. And go to school. And that was what life was.

But what would happen if nobody stopped those dumb thoughts? If maybe instead of having consequences, everything I did got rewarded? If the dumber I got, the more successful I became?

We are living in a teenager's wet dream. A white

male teenager. He needs to be ignored. He is just a distraction. Vote him out in November.

We need to demand that we defund the Police Union. All policing. Redirect those funds to teachers and social workers. Remove guns from police. End mandatory sentencing for non-violent crimes. I don't know, make a national data-base that flags violent cops. Change laws that give immunity to police brutality. Make it easier to sue the police department. I don't even know. Psychology tests for cops. End for-profit prisons.

I don't even know. The list is forever. Abolish ICE.

And while you are at it, pull yourself up by the boot-straps, and get a job at Amazon. They are hiring.

As long as you don't have a fever.

DAY EIGHTY

Stocks way up. The new theory is that things will eventually get better. Maybe not in a year, or two years, or ten years, but eventually, and so if these billion dollar companies can just hold out for a decade or so, things will be just fine. Which makes me want to punch somebody. For one thing, it is probably true, nothing matters and the rich will just stay rich and the rest of us can just eat a bag of dog shit. And two. nothing will ever change, ever. That is, unless we put progressives in charge. Get money out of politics. Have sweeping, and long-lasting reform.

In other news, the Orange Douche wasn't hiding out in his bunker, he was just doing a site survey. Making sure everything was up to code, et cetera. It was all just a giant co-inky-dink. No cowardice. Just a smart businessman using his vast construction knowledge to make sure everything was ship-shape.

In other news, all four of the police officers involved in killing George Floyd have now been charged. If you think protests don't work, you are wrong. They work. They need to continue.

In other news, the bagels turned out great.

In other news, today is Wednesday. If everything works out right, we will be on the road by Sunday.

In other news, the exhaustion is total. Went to leave today, to go to a protest at 3p, sudden downpour. All weather forecasts predicted rain for the rest of the day. Hour walk there. Protest in the rain. Hour walk back. My shoes have huge holes. Assumed the thing was going to get cancelled. The idea of walking in the rain for two hours seemed insane. An hour later, the rain stopped. Then it was the opposite of rain. Clearest skies in days. But now what? Show up two hours late to a thing I thought was going to be cancelled in the first place? I don't know. This feeling of urgency combined with this feeling of frustration? Every day now, for eighty days?

In other news, Status Cuomo called the head of the Police Union in New York and apologized for saying anything bad about police. He didn't mean it. It was all politics. Oh, and he did it in secret.

In other news, I told Professor Curly that one nice thing about having a car is that I could buy beer in bulk. She made a frowny face. Said she thought I was going the way of Kate Moss. Full sober. At that point it was me that made a frowny face.

In other news, smoking is once again good for you. With respect to Coronavirus. I wonder how they do these studies. Who volunteers? What is your control group? I mean, normally, in normal times, you have a hypothesis and then you do experiments to prove it, or disprove it, but these ain't normal times. And I don't think it is the science that I am questioning. It's the data. And where is it coming from? Do they question people who have the virus? Like, does anyone you are in contact with smoke? And if yes, do they then monitor the person who smokes to see if they get the virus? I guess I could read the studies, but they all seem to be published in the Daily Mail, so I am not so sure I would trust them anyway.

In other news, here is a list of how to reduce police killings by 72%:

1. Require officers to de-escalate situations, where possible, by communicating with subjects, maintaining distance, and otherwise eliminating the need to use force

2. Don't allow officers to choke or strangle civilians, in many cases where less lethal force could be used instead, resulting in the unnecessary death or serious injury of civilians

3. Require officers to intervene and stop excessive force used by other officers and report these incidents immediately to a

supervisor

4. Restrict officers from shooting at moving vehicles, which is regarded as a particularly dangerous and ineffective tactic

5. Develop a Force Continuum that limits the types of force and/or weapons that can be used to respond to specific types of resistance

6. Require officers to exhaust all other reasonable means before resorting to deadly force

7. Require officers to give a verbal warning, when possible, before shooting at a civilian

8. Require officers to report each time they use force or threaten to use force against civilians

In other news, Professor Curly is pregnant! Just joking. It is all bagel weight. Plus, she is on the block, so I only chuck it in her dumper.

In other news, Justin Trudeau just did a press conference in blackface to show solidarity with Black Lives Matter. Just joking. He did have a nice beard though. And his buns, [21 seconds later] are fantastic!

In other news, more people have been arrested for protesting since the murder of George Floyd than all the people arrested for white collar crimes in all of 2019.

In other news, protesters broke into a fancy car dealership in lower Manhattan, stole 80 cars, and then proceeded to drive the cars to high-end fashion shops and loot them. I am not so sure about the reporting on this, but I don't care. I really, really, like the idea. Plus, there is that dealership on Canal Street and Avenue of the Americas, so there is some possible credulity to the story.

In other news, **Democracy Now!** played a rap song by George Floyd in between one of their segments today. It was quite good. And because we live in what can only be called a Meta-Satire, all I could think about was the Onion article:

Black Man Blissfully Unaware His Name Going To Be Hashtag By End Of Week

Which was profoundly unsettling.

In other news, do you think Laura Bush and Dick Cheney boned when they were in the bunker under the White House during 9/11? I mean, she seems like she fucks, and I have seen images of Dick's bulge. Plus, scary times. Plus, I Am The Decider In Chief was busy looking for cowards, elsewhere.

In other news, does anyone want to house sit? I have a t-shirt package coming soon. And the plants. And the other mails. There was that one rat that tried to bite me, only, and the apartment is close to the subway. Good light. Two air conditioners. A freezer full of New England Steamers. And! yesterday we got another 20-pack of toilet paper. You could wipe your ass for days without even making a dent! No bunker though.

In other news, if money doesn't matter, and the only thing that matters is spending money, and by spending money you maintain the economy, why the fuck don't people like Jeff Bezos, or Bill Gates, or Tim Apple just give people money to buy things? I am serious. I really don't think people just want to sit around in their apartments doing nothing, so I think work, whatever that is, would always be done, and whatever, even if you didn't want to work, who cares? Is reality just a big joke? Like God is waiting for us to say, Hey! wait a minute! If nothing I do really matters, and things will just be fine regardless, and as long as I keep taking this useless paper thing, and give it to this other useless metal thing, but also get up in the morning, and ride on a train for a while, and then sit around for a while, and then go have dinner with my family, everything will be just fine? And then suddenly we all just transcend. And God goes:

Ha! Jokes on you! I thought you idiots understood when I had you build the pyramids! Everything is just infrastructure! The moment you start to pull apart everything is chaos! I even gave you a name for it! Seth! The Harbinger of Chaos! Oh! Ha! What a bunch of buffoons!

In other news, I now know how ***Ruiner*** will end.

In other news, ***Ruiner*** has been renamed ***Kartouche***. [Lawsuit pending]

In other news, it started raining again.

No way I am going to protests now, it is well past curfew.

DAY EIGHTY-ONE

Stocks kind of down. 2 million more new UnEmployment claims bringing the total to 42 million. 110,000 American deaths from the Coronavirus. Protests in every American city in relation to racist police murders and systemic racism. The President threatening to send in the military to stop the protests.

Autopsy reveals that George Floyd had the Coronavirus at some point. Which the Republicans say is the one, and only, proven death from the virus.

Professor Curly and I went to a protest. Prospect Park. Thousands of people. I only saw one person not wearing a mask. A man, naturally. People were handing out masks, water, snacks. Very peaceful. Professor Curly had a sign that read, DEFUND THE POLICE. I had a sign that said, BUNKER BOI. Which wasn't the best sign to be holding. I thought it would have more of a protest vibe. The vibe was not that. The vibe was closer to funeral. I didn't get beat down or anything. But the sign was inappropriate. Like that time I made a last minute costume for trick or treating in Bed Stuy one year. I thought I would be a spooky ghost. I cut some holes in a white sheet. Bed Stuy is something like 90% black. I wasn't trying to be funny. I was just short-sighted and stupid. I didn't wear it for very long before I realized how dumb it was. I took it off.

But BUNKER BOI. I mean, I understand that it is not enough to just defeat Donald Trump right now. I also understand that it is not enough to just be pissed off right now. The reason that Bernie is far superior to Biden is this exact argument. There is no Both Sides. There is the left, which is a canary in a coal mine, and the right, which is the Klu Klux Klan sitting on tops of Trillions of dollars.

I mean, think about it. The Orange Douche got impeached for forcing a foreign country to interfere in an American election, has bungled a response to a global pandemic that has caused the deaths of over 100,000 Americans, has no plan to pull us out of the worst economic calamity since the Great Depression aside from just telling us all to get back to work, who cares if you die, and his approval rating has dropped what? 1 percent?

Yes, obviously it is not just him. But that is the point! We need everyone out! Every both sides, reach across the aisle, can't we all just get along and ignore the problem mother fuckers out!

Which is voting. Which is protests. Which is white guilt. Black anger. Suburban moms. "Swing" vote nonsense. Never Biden. Whatever it is that makes you say, It is not enough, it doesn't matter. All hands on deck!

Vote progressive. Vote local. Vote always.

I have to say, my new bagel recipe is top notch. No egg-wash. No foolish soup. I flip the bagels halfway through, so they cook evenly on both sides. No secret ingredients. I think I might be onto something!

Lazy J Bagels is back!

I guess I should make a batch for Sunday. For Professor Curly's dad and mom and step-mom and Scott and Miette and Grit and Sea-Bass. Need flour.

Here is the new plan. We get up on Sunday. Or, well, George Orwell, Animal Farm! He says as the tourettes kicks in. Or, well, Professor Curly gets up on Sunday. Goes and gets the rental car. Drives back to the apartment. We load up our gear. And plants. Drive into the city. Go to the Hole. Pick up a mixer for Scott. Drive for five hours to New Hampshire. Drop the rental off. Have dinner with Dick and Kathy. Cathy. Stay the night at a hotel. On Dick's dime. Get up the next morning. Get the new car. Go to the grocery in New Hampshire. Drive two hours to Vermont. Go immediately to the cabin and hunker down. This time with fresh air and better politics.

There are few details that need to be sussed out, but it is looking pretty good.

Then we stay there for a while. I either go to work, or the work gets postponed. Then we come back to the city. Refreshed with a new exhaustion.

And a new car.

Thanks, Bob Barker.

DAY EIGHTY-TWO

Stocks way up. Everything the same. Except some fishy jobs numbers. Which, a couple months ago I probably would have trusted. With reservations. But now? During this precise moment of time? And words like, Shocking jobs numbers! used to describe how surprised the government was that there were Jobs gains in May. Maybe there was. But it shouldn't be surprising to anyone if it is true. This isn't the fucking Oscars. And for the stock market to go up the way it did today, with a supposed new jobs claim of 2 million, and for the stock market to barely move yesterday with an actual new UnEmployment declaration of that same number. 2 million. You see what I mean by fishy? My guess is they cooked the books. Claimed a victory. When people find out about it it will be too late. And that is the world we are living in now.

What can you do? It will all trickle down anyway. All we have to do now is wait.

Professor Curly got tested today. Results in

three to five days. Did both tests. For the virus, and for antibodies. Not really sure what to do with the information when we get it. Or how we are supposed to behave until we get it. Or if that means she is now on some sort of database. But she did the test. However, whatever. There were 1,200 reported deaths today so far. But if you bothered to read the news you would think that the pandemic is over. Which ties into the fishy jobs report. As long as people aren't actively dying on the street, and as long as there isn't a homeless encampment out on your sidewalk, we are just supposed to believe whatever they tell us to believe. Which depends on what your definition of is, is.

Fried Chicken Gizzards in the afternoon. For myself. I didn't even bother to include Professor Curly. She had pasta and salad for dinner. Secret ingredient? Love. And crunchy pig skin from the carnitas.

Tomorrow should be intense. Supposed to be hot. 86F. Muggy. Need to pack. Make bagels. Clean the apartment. Take the air conditioner down. Cut that fucking branch off. Make lunches and snacks for the trip. Would like to go to a march. I think there will be some very intense, very large ones tomorrow. But it might not be possible. And it might not be smart. Like I said though, yesterday there was one, ONE person that didn't wear a mask at the rally. And the risk of infection drops by 80% if everyone is wearing a mask. And that is with respect to indoor transmission. I think it drops to nearly 0% outdoors if everyone is wearing a mask. I should do some more research. But it may just be a dumb risky move considering we are about to travel places of minimal exposure due to a lesser populace.

I don't know what to say. I guess this is goodbye. Tomorrow is the last of it. I have some sentimental desire to coalesce all these thoughts into one big picture. I mean, it has been a dark, hilarious, tasty, and fantastic ride. Milestones. Perspective changes. Bonin'.

Have we learned anything? I learned how to make bagels pretty good. This last batch was by far the best. You can't take that away from me.

We have learned that nothing will ever change. That there are two sets of rules. One for the wealthy, and those in power, and a second set for everybody else. But we knew that before. Try again. Fail again. Fail better. But then you look up images of Samuel Beckett, and he is holding a Gucci bag. So, sigh. Then forget it was him that said it.

We have learned that Schrodinger designed our economy. That supply is a construct, and demand is a slight of hand trick intended to fool us into thinking we have choices when in fact no choice actually exists.

We have learned that it is possible to live in a 1 ½ bedroom apartment with two people without any possible outlet for over eighty days. Not recommended, but possible.

We have learned that structure, and self discipline is essential to success in times of adversity. That chaos leads to more chaos, and unrest.

We learned first hand that the rats were starving.

I don't even know. I mean, I guess we learned things. I learned that I am gullible. I thought we could pull this off. Honestly. That we would pull together. Understand the consequences. Err towards science, and hunker down, and I don't know, come out ahead. But selfishness prevails. On one hand. And reality prevails on the other. And I guess I just need to accept that.

The Fuddrucker Rebellion and the Florida beach parties put everybody at risk for no reason. Should be stopped.

The Black Lives Matter protests need to happen. Puts everybody at risk. Should NOT be stopped.

The Racist Republican Right is about to find science again. And it is going to suck. Because the corporate media will amplify it in order to make money. We need to brace for this. There will be a new resurgence of the virus. They will point to protests. Blame the Libs. The blacks. Et al. Et cetera.

But those are the risks we are up against. Racist Liars Who Only Care About Money. They will lie and lie and lie. And the New York Times will both sides it. The Washington Post will both sides it. AP news will both sides it. CNN will both sides it. MSNBC will both sides it. And it will be attrition. And attrition. And attrition. They'll keep calling me, they'll keep calling me, I won't go, I won't go. But in the end we will all go.

Unless we say, No! these are all lies. You are lying to me. The Republican party is lying to me. The President is lying to me. The Attorney General is lying to me. It will never stop.

But whatever. Nobody has that much self discipline. I hate the Orange Douche so much, and think if we give him four more years that will end America forever, that I would crawl over starving babies tangled in barbed wire floating in a pit of sulfuric acid to vote him out.

And so it is.

Tomorrow I am mailing back my primary ballot. Voted Bernie. Professor Curly did too. Hope it helps. Was nice to have the option. Still uncertain as to why they tried to cancel the primary. The amount of damage that is going to cause in November. Doesn't seem worth it. And it is two-fold. Trump wins, and we are all fucked. Or Biden wins, and half the Democratic party becomes 3rd party again. I mean, we are not going to suddenly see the light that health care should not be tied to employment. That corporations are not good for small businesses. That landlords should not have more rights than the tenants they are using to pay their taxes. Tom Perez is a fucking moron. The DNC is a bunch of idiots.

Well, I didn't mean to go on that diatribe, but what can you do?

Oh, think twice. It's another day for you and me in paradise.

Phil Collins. Remember him? He really stuck it to Ronald Reagan in that one video.

Watch, ***This Is America***, by Childish Gambino.

A little bit of a different tone.

DAY EIGHTY-THREE

[Pre-dendum. This work was always meant to be a daily report on what I assumed would be a six-week isolation from the outside world. How me and Professor Curly navigated the isolation. I had always intended to finish the reporting on the first day when I felt comfortable enough to return to the ashes of what was regular life. Supposedly on Monday, June 8th, 2020, they are going to end the restrictions between the states of New York, Maine, New Hampshire, Connecticut, and Rhode Island. Which probably means I will head back to work on the 15th of June. Aside from Day Four, when I went to Jack's studio, which was also the first day the lockdown officially started for New York City, this is an accurate accounting of events from my perspective. Of Eighty-Three days of isolation. This is meant as a work of art. And therefore this will be the ultimate entry. Stay safe, stay thirsty, and may god have mercy on your soul.]

Last day. Made sixteen bagels. Eight plain, eight

everything. Cleaned the bathroom. Professor Curly packed. Cleaned her office, and the living room. Sent in our absentee ballots. Forgot to take the air conditioner down. Tomorrow. Didn't cut the tree branch. Not sure that will ever happen.

Jess said he would take the plants for us. Jim is going to grab the mixer for Scott. Pick it up in the morning. Professor Curly will go get the rental at 9a. I still need to pack. Make lunches. Unplug everything. On the road by 11a. Hopefully.

Two things I forgot to mention. One, when me, and Professor Curly were walking to the protests on Thursday, I yelled at her the way that you yell at people when you are inside and have been inside with each other for weeks at a time, but on the street. Use your inside voice! style. Which was funny, but embarrassing. You probably shouldn't yell at people in general, but it came out so fast. It seems shame is something that gets lost when you have no frame of reference.

Which brings me to the second thing. I was telling Professor Curly a story about electronic mails, while making her some popcorn for a snack. I was trying to explain how many mails I got from my bandmates about some songs that Michael was mixing. Halfway through the story I followed her into her office to finish, and she stopped me from telling her the story, and asked me, So, are you not going to make me any popcorn? No interest in the story. At all. I think I said something like, Well, fuck you, why don't you make your own fucking popcorn, your highness. But just then the popcorn started to pop, so I had to run into the kitchen, and make sure it didn't burn.

I mean, aside from being a couple of dicks all the time, I think we came out pretty good after all of this. Relationship-wise. Which is good to know. Although, remember when I was trying to turn this into a murder/mystery? And it didn't go over so well? I did have a new idea. For a short story.

This guy gets trapped in a cabin with his lady friend, and winter is coming in pretty fast. He realizes that they don't have enough food for both of them to last the winter, so he hatches a plan. He is going to fatten his lady friend up with the food that they have, and when they run out, he will kill her, and live off of her body for the rest of the winter. But when the food runs out, he is skin and bones. He goes to choke his lady friend to death, but his fingers won't reach around her neck because it is so fat. And the last scene is her just laughing and laughing and laughing while he tries to choke her.

Jack Sprat's Miscalculation.

Dried beans. A gallon of black beans. Baking needs. Plenty of bacon grease. The fridge is almost completely empty. A bag of sugar. Two boxes of spaghetti. A couple sticks of butter. Two full ice trays. The cupboards are essentially bare. I guess when the second wave hits we will have to do this all over again. I already feel poor. Going back to work seems ominous. What can you do?

There was a retraction about how the jobs numbers were not what they seemed. One day later. But nobody reported on it. The propaganda succeeded. And then the Orange Douche said something like, George Floyd is looking down on us, happy about these numbers. It's a good day for him. A good day for America.

Meta-Satire.

Cook the books. Jack the stock market. Claim a victory. Say one of the stupidest things possible. Move on to something else. Works every single fucking time.

But whatever. I will claim UnEmployment tomorrow. Hope for the best. Then again next Sunday. And I guess that will be it. Back to work. Nothing has changed. No testing. No contact tracing. Nothing different. Just now we have to go back to work. Watch it all happen all over again. Except this time there will be no help.

Cecina tacos for dinner. Flour torts. With black beans ots. On The Side. For all you assholes that have never worked a restaurant job.

My avocado seed never sprouted. Rooted? Not sure what to do with it. I still have hope. I just don't know if I have done anything wrong. I followed all the directions. It is over a month now. I think. Time is like a boner you wake up with.

It has always been there. You don't know what caused it. You don't know what to do with it. But it is impossible to ignore.

You can ignore an avocado seed. From the outside. Boring as hell.

Well, this is the final goodbye. I should have got better beer for this party. And the chips are for the car ride. But I think there may be some ice cream left. Cookie dough. I have two frozen burritos to eat tonight before I go to bed, and some nacho cheese and sour cream. But I think that is it.

Coffee is made for the morning. Bags are mostly packed. I got my tools, and some toothpaste. A toothbrush. Nothing to look forward to, except open wounds and open roads.

To thine own selves, be righteous.

JT 06/06/2020

ACKNOWLEDGMENTS

Miette Gillette
Tina Satter
George Truman
Peggy Truman
Scott Gillette
Jack Warren
Michael Jung
Jess Barbagallo
Mariana Catalina

ABOUT THE AUTHOR

Joey Truman is a writer and artist based in New York City. He performs with the bands UM, Escalators, Bronko Dilater, and Soft Inserts. His upcoming books from Whisk(e)y Tit include **Ruiner**, a book about bees, and **Movable Rooms**, a book about dwelling.

Other titles by Joey Truman:
Postal Child (2016)
Killing the Math (2016)
KinderRinder (2017)
Parlay (2018)
Cooking Cockroach (2019)
Killing the Math 2 (2019)
Etiquette (2020)

ABOUT THE PUBLISHER

Whisk(e)y Tit is committed to restoring degradation and degeneracy to the literary arts. We work with authors who are unwilling to sacrifice intellectual rigor, unrelenting playfulness, and visual beauty in our literary pursuits, often leading to texts that would otherwise be abandoned in today's largely homogenized literary landscape. In a world governed by idiocy, our commitment to these principles is an act of civil service and civil disobedience alike.

www.ingramcontent.com/pod-product-compliance
Lightning Source LLC
Chambersburg PA
CBHW062032120526
44592CB00036B/1854